BOOKS searching for AUTHORS

Children communicating through the writing and visual process

Paul Johnson

Hodder & Stoughton

A MEMBER OF THE HODDER HEADLINE GROUP

Contents

To Beryl Edwards
who first showed me what the making of books
can do for young children.

Cataloguing in Publication Data is available from the British Library.

ISBN 0 340 58910 8

First published 1994
Impression number   10   9   8   7   6   5   4   3   2   1
Year   1998   1997   1996   1995   1994

© 1994 Paul Johnson

Typeset by Litho Link Ltd, Welshpool, Powys.
Printed in Great Britain for Hodder & Stoughton Educational, a division of Hodder Headline PLC, Mill Road, Dunton Green, Sevenoaks, Kent TN13 2YA by Scotprint Ltd.

About this book

Books Searching for Authors has developed out of Paul Johnson's best-selling book on children making books, A Book of One's Own (published by Hodder and Stoughton 1990) and Literacy Through the Book Arts (published by Hodder and Stoughton 1993). Although it is not necessary to have read his previous books for Books Searching for Authors to be intelligible, it would certainly assist the reader's understanding of the book art approach to writing and visual communication to have done so.

In Books Searching for Authors Paul Johnson continues the search for new book forms made from single sheets of paper, requiring, for the most part, only a pair of scissors and a craft knife, and develops the ideas from his previous books. Most of these book forms have a Zen simplicity about them, but the opportunities they create for the exploration and synthesis of ideas expressed in words, pictures and diagrams are endless. If you have not already been converted to the book arts, either as teacher or parent, you will be by the end of this book!

 # Acknowledgments

The author and publishers would like to thank the following for permission to quote from copyright material: William Heinemann Ltd and Reed International Books for extracts from The Jolly Postman by J. and A. Ahlberg; Abner Stein and Jonathan Cape for extracts from Sam's Sandwich by David Pelham; Marie Claire for the right to reproduce page 83 of the July 1992 issue, reproduced with kind permission of Marie Claire/ European Magazines 1991 Ltd/Robert Harding Syndication; Faber and Faber Ltd for an eight line excerpt from Night Mail III by W. H. Auden; Blackie Children's Books for extracts from Noisy Norman by B. Kaiser and M. Wells; Orchard Books and The Watts Group for extracts from A Book of Boxes by Laura Mason; and Pan Books Ltd for excerpts from Cleanaway! by N. Salaman.

We are indebted to the following schools for giving permission to reproduce the work of their pupils: Beaver Road Infant School, Manchester; Beaver Road Junior School, Manchester; Cavendish Road Primary School, Manchester; Christ Church Primary School, Chadderton; Christ the King RC Primary School, Manchester; Miles Platting Primary School, Manchester; Mills Hill Primary School, Oldham; Norbury Hall Primary School, Stockport; St Augustine's CE Primary School, Manchester; St George's CE Infant School, Stockport; St Joseph's Infant School, Stockport; Urmston Infant School, Trafford; Whitfield Primary School, Glossop.

A special thanks to Lorraine Davies, Rosemary Jeffries, Vanessa Kershaw and Patricia Locke, whose inspired teaching and belief in the book arts made my task so much easier.

My thanks also to Helen Philips and Sally Kemp for allowing me to reproduce their visual aids; Roisin Brolly for reproducing her daughter's work, and a special thanks to Ercelia James for allowing me free access to her unrivalled treasure house of stimulating book art material; also to Jean Berloff for allowing me to reproduce his work.

Finally, my indebtedness to Judith and Mac for spotting all my grammatical shortcomings.

The chapter 'Children's Books as Architecture' first appeared in truncated form in Children's Literature in Education, volume 23, number 3.

Learning comes when we turn over an experience in our mind; we begin to think about it, and usually we want to tell somebody about it – a friend – to explain, relive it, select from it, evaluate it and gradually absorb it, assimilate it, digest it – until it has become part of our ourselves, lasting forever. All lasting learning is a becoming.

Christian Schiller

● *Introduction*

'I've lost my book,' said Tracy.
'Where did you see it last?' came the reply.
'No, I mean I've lost the ideas in my head I had for it.'

Books and authors searching for each other

Before sending this book to the publisher I wrestled with the title. Should it be *Books Searching for Authors* or *Authors Searching for Books*? Both seemed appropriate. Was it the book that enabled authors to *become*? Indeed, without book concepts of one kind or another, would there ever have been such people, even in embryonic form? Or did the insatiable need to communicate through symbolic marks inscribed on a surface force the book – like a miraculous act of creation – into 'being'. History is littered with these chicken and egg puzzles. Did Beethoven elevate the symphony, or the symphony elevate Beethoven?

It is impossible to discuss almost any facet of the development of communication in general, and literacy in particular, without reference to the book form, yet, historically, this has been the case, at least in education. That is why my concern is not so much with the *what* of children's writing, but the *how* of their writing. And *how* they write within the context of writing *as design*. Of course it is

impossible for the *how* to stand apart from the *what*, but the 'environment' of words on paper has never been seen as that important. The curriculum habitually detaches writing in whichever form (including the computer), or to whatever ends, from the language of the page (or screen), it is written on.

Does a blank page have a language? To the book designer it is that rectangular phenomenon we call the page which is the oxygen of visually communicated language. And without words, or visual images the page as a concept does not exist. One is inextricably bound up with the other. Without the other neither exists. So whether one starts with the idea of the writer, or the idea of the book, one concept must embrace the other for there to be any meaningful communication. The multiplicity of communication forms today demands that the writer is a 'designer of words'.

The marginalisation of the book form in the literary continuum is one of the greatest disservices that has been done to our children.

But this myopia is not one-sided. Even the nineties have seen the appearance of elaborately designed, full-colour books on 'bookcraft' for children. Some even venture into model page grid designs and novel ways of making collage

illustrations, but none of them show children's work or discuss how the book artist, at developmental stages of communicating, assembles ideas through the layers of folded paper that comprise the book form. It is like giving someone a new car which is complete in every way except that it has no engine! This travesty is compounded by the fact that the innovative children's picture books of today are just waiting to be used as vehicles of learning in areas as diverse as narrative and non-narrative forms of writing, paper technology, illustration, and design. Ironically, both kinds of books sit side-by-side on shop and library bookshelves but, like many a marriage, there is no communication between them. It is not that communication has broken down – there was never any there in the first place.

So many important changes have evolved in the book concept in general and children's books in particular over the last decade or so that it would be impossible to even attempt to define them in one book. What I have tried to do here is to discuss two aspects of those innovative developments and then show, essentially through children's work and the means by which that work was processed, how pupils' communication skills can be enhanced in the curriculum through similar constructions.

The first of these is the astonishing transformation of the book from the solid, somewhat inert, three-dimensional form largely unchanged for two thousand years, to the multi-dimensional 'architectural' proliferations of the last ten years or so. These changes have taken place almost exclusively in children's publishing. The other is the increasing minimalisation of words in print and the rising status of visually-communicated concepts. On the surface both these aspects – books as architecture, diminishing words/expanding pictures – seem disparate, but as the children's work shows, they are, in fact, closely related, for the architectural nature of the book reorientates the way verbal and visual ideas are communicated. It is too early to say where these new developments in the book form are going, or how they will change the way that not only children, but indeed all of us, will learn to communicate in the future. What is certain is that rapid changes are taking place, not just in books, but the whole communications industry, and that for education to assume – as it so often does – that such things lie beyond the boundaries of the curriculum concept is naively counterproductive to the needs of present and future generations.

In some areas of communication words have almost become an endangered species. From minimalist captions in the advertisements we now regularly have wordless ones – and further, large hoardings which contain almost nothing at all except a cryptic visual message. Yet is that which is communicated minimal? I think not. These designs are switching us over to another kind of perceiving and decoding; one which is not only

wholly visual, but dependent on the reader's retrieval of, and interaction with, stored images. It is a subtle psychology and is linked to what Margaret Meek (1988) has to say in the context of the multi-layering of children's picture books and the influence of environmental print on reading. Indeed, it is often towards children that these forms of communication are directed. Has education even begun to assess the implications of such things in how pupils learn to communicate in a rapidly changing information-orientated environment?

I have called the influence of these changes on the way we teach children to learn *communicating through the writing and visual process*, because the singularity of conventional literacy models will not do any more. Books, magazines, the artefacts of the communications industry (even junk mail) demand that the eyes do more than merely scan words for meaning. The current interest in children *reading* the pictures in their books is the beginning of what must be a lengthy reappraisal of the role of the intelligent eye in thought and processed action. Of course art educators have been saying this for over half a century – admittedly in often narrowly defined fine art-oriented ways – but it is only recently that the influential literacy fraternity has sat up and taken notice of it. It is beginning to dawn on all those engaged in the teaching process that written words do not constitute an isolated hierarchical symbology, but are an important part of a visual language. The mind is continually confronted with a barrage of visually communicated images and the task of making sense of them.

Close encounters of the third dimension

I had the good fortune to go to art school and, unlike most students today, we were encouraged to diversify. On Monday and Tuesday we painted, Wednesday was given over to art history, and on Thursday and Friday, we learnt sculpture. So it was that two- and three-dimensional art was experienced side-by-side. Both seemed to cross over so often: one found solutions to drawing problems through stone carving (the chisel is not unlike a pencil); and the flowing, plastic forming of clay modelling was illuminated by pen and ink work. Whether one was dealing with the illusion of space in a painting, or the making of spatial forms in clay or plaster, the mind was being stretched in a way which would have been impossible without that pedagogical training. Spending so much of my life in a relationship with paper, a material which can be flat at one moment and spatial the next, I find that that experience of thirty years ago is invaluable to me.

Three-dimensional art has always been neglected in favour of the 2D kind (I have more to say about this presently) and so in schooling, children, who generally have a curate's egg art education, tend to miss out on the third dimension. The more I am immersed in explorations of the book, and how children learn through them, the more I am aware of our inability to think in an interrelated 2D/3D way. How often are viewers ('readers' is hardly the correct term) aware, when moving through a pop-up book, that they are looking primarily at sculpture, and that some images are 2D illusions of reality (the surface artwork of the un-engineered page), and others (the engineered pop-up forms) 3D illusions of reality. In the pop-up book *The Dwindling Party* (Gorey, 1982), the engineered characters show their frontal imagery on one side, and their back views on the rear. In *Great Buildings of the World* (Smith, 1984), the pop-up Eiffel Tower rises from the centre of the page not as a single form with artwork on both sides, but as a 360 degree spatial form, so the onlooker sees the engineering architecture of that creation just as one would inspect it *in situ*. When children open out the onion and cucumber slices in *Sam's Sandwich* (Pelham, 1990), or remove the letters from *The Jolly Postman* (Ahlberg and Ahlberg 1986), they are handling forms which are at one and the same time 3D 'realities', and illusions of that reality because they are all merely constructed from paper.

All these examples of multi-dimensional image-making place children in a new area of perceiving reality, inventing and expressing through it. Marks on paper have blossomed out into a host of other ways of assimilating and communicating information. And what changes will visual words experience, collaborating, as they do in so many complex ways, with these new visual forms?

So to be successful teachers we all need to become sculptors – or as I will describe it later, architects – to define these new writing and image-making processes. It is, I believe, one of the most exciting and, dare I say, enjoyable challenges in modern education history.

1 *Children's books as architecture*

We look at a picture, but in a book. That subtle distinction has more meaning for education than we know.

A visit to almost any bookshop in the country during the early nineties couldn't fail to impress upon one that *The Jolly Postman* by Janet and Allan Ahlberg, had done for children's books in recent years what 'The Beatles' did for popular music in the sixties. It caught the nation's imagination and became a cultural symbol of our times; for as parents we give our children and as teachers our pupils, what we think as being, not only the best of a particular genre, but what is most *significant*.

But why has a book containing letters, advertisements and postcards in envelopes stood out in this way against a vast landscape of so many new book concepts for children? Late 1991 saw the arrival of *The Jolly Christmas Postman* as a sequel to its illustrious forebear – a fatter book this time, with more than just letters and the like to take out and read, like a jigsaw puzzle and a pop-up 'peep' show. Are we on the verge of a Jolly Postman saga, with 'The Jolly Easter Postman' around the corner, to be followed by 'The Jolly Postman in Disneyland/New York/Paris/Berlin/Bangkok'? The mind boggles at what objects will be contained in those envelopes! Like that other popular British postman, Postman Pat, there seems to be a lot of creative potential going for that particular occupation.

When *The Jolly Postman* was first published in 1986 it was a landmark in children's publishing. Lots of other story books had included correspondence between characters, indeed it is only natural that it should be so, as the letter form is the most common personal communication

The Jolly Postman *by J. and A. Ahlberg (Heinemann, 1986)*

system of all. But the presence of real-looking, yet delightfully fanciful envelopes containing equally genuine, yet humorously concocted mail had a flavour of compelling originality. And its success was not due only to that, but also because it had arrived at a time when a charismatic figurehead was desperately needed to symbolise what was being achieved in children's books in that decade.

Alongside the Jolly Postman books in the early nineties was another book, eagerly attempting to compete with them in popularity. David Pelham's *Sam's Sandwich*, although having no removable parts, broke new ground in invention. The book's cover replicates, in folded paper, a wholemeal sandwich (in the health-conscious nineties it would be unthinkable to have white bread). Inside, lettuce, tomatoes, watercress, cucumber, cheese, egg, salami and onion are layered in

Sam's Sandwich *by D. Pelham (Jonathan Cape, 1990)*

sequences of open-out paper forms. The story is told through the horrible creepy crawlies that Sam places in the sandwich, and the macabre delight he experiences as his sister eats her way through it! A stroke of genius is the packaging of the book in a brown paper bag, just as if one were buying it as a salad bar sandwich. So a new 'accessing' task is encountered here. The book must be removed from the paper bag rather like expensive private press books have to be removed from their slipcases. Their prime role is to protect the valuable object inside, but the slipcase has symbolic status too, for it heralds the book's status, adding another layer of preciousness to that symbolised by the book's hard cover. In this context the 'book' (as contents) has become the sacrament reached by progressing through successive ante-chambers: one is being 'prepared'. Here a common paper bag, so common that like many low status paper objects it is brown in colour, has been elevated by its 'preparing' function. At one and the same time it is both part of the joke surrounding Sam's sandwich as a worthless paper bag, and a quasi–religious doorway through which we must pass to reach the book. One would never dream of throwing the bag away, for it is part of the book's status, indeed, as I have experienced, those who have purchased it from book stores which sell it minus the bag have felt cheated when they discover that their purchase is not complete. As the reader opens the sandwich, the contents are lifted from the inert compactness of the closed book-sandwich into 3D reality. When all the ingredients have been projected in this way, the sandwich stands as a complex paper sculpture which can be viewed from several different viewpoints or held in a number of ways.

As with *The Jolly Postman*, it was inevitable that a sequel would follow *Sam's Sandwich*. In *Sam's Surprise* (Pelham, 1992), Sam's sister Samantha gets her own back by giving him a box of chocolates with 'nasties' hidden inside them. One by one the chocolates are removed by Sam's friends, until only the remnants of protective wrappers are left in the bottom of the box. These are 'real' shreds of paper and not 'painted on' ones. Here, a wrapped box replaces slices of bread, and layers of chocolate substitute salad, eggs and meat. The layers are all the same shape and size, and so lack the variety of form which is so compelling about *Sam's Sandwich*. However, while many children's books are about boxes and their contents, it is innovatory for the paper technology of the book form to be a real box. It shows, again, a move towards books simulating 3D reality, rather than a 2D illusion of it, which typifies children's books of the late-twentieth century. Time will tell if *Sam's Surprise* will match the success of its predecessor.

And these books are not isolated cases. Here are just a few of many other children's books which are essentially three-dimensional in concept.

Noisy Norman (Kaiser and Wells, 1986) opens up to make a free-standing motor vehicle which is lifted and slotted into a 3D form. Diagrams show how it is folded down again. The inside back cover of the book houses the accompanying story, which pulls out as a concertina (see opposite).

In a different sculptural vein, the nursery rhyme *There was an old lady who swallowed a fly* (Adams, 1973) is told through a series of enlarging holes cut into the pages. On the last page we see all the creatures the old lady has swallowed, and through the facing page, the rhyme is read through all the layers of diminishing pages. Watching children experiencing this book, you see that it is the negative holes which are the most significant thing about it, not only because the hole is a culture shock, but because the reader soon discovers that they get progressively bigger and so the spatial expectation – so much part of the subject matter – is inextricably part of understanding the plot. Later, I describe this kind of book (there are several

Noisy Norman *by B. Kaiser and M. Wells (Blackie, 1986)*

like it) as *à la* Barbara Hepworth sculpture, for in both, negative spaces are part of the overall concept of form.

The *Alf* books (Ruth-Stephens and Enik, 1988) use the book form in another kinesthetically 3D way. In *Alf Hides Out* (1988), Alf, the bear-like protagonist, is detachable from the book and fastened to a length of wool. As the pages are turned, slots are provided on the page for him to hide in (to be placed in by the reader) while he is being hunted by Brian. So there is only one image of Alf which is moved through the book by the reader as the story is read, although 'performed' might be a better word to describe the process. None of the pages has anything but items of furniture or cupboards. The reader provides his or her own answers as to whether or not Alf is small enough to hide in the slots provided.

The three-dimensional book

Now there is nothing new about 3D books. Pop-up books have been with us for a surprisingly long time. The pop-up toy theatre, so popular in the 19th century, can be traced back, in concept at least, to 'turn-up' books which began to appear in London at around 1765. In the 20th century, the right-angled 90 degree book which so fascinated Victorian children, developed into the 180 degree book which opens out flat on a table top. Today they cover every conceivable subject from the human body to astronomy, with Raymond Briggs' evergreen, *Fungus the Bogeyman* (Briggs, 1982) representing a whole genre of pop-up story books. Some of the most startling of this family of 3D

books are in an adult mode. *The Working Camera* (Hedgecoe and Van Der Meer, 1985) is a feat of engineering ingenuity, almost matching that of the camera itself. It shows, with far greater clarity than a book of diagrams could, the function of the SLR camera, the design of the lens, and how to light and compose photographic subjects. The 3D reality of the paper engineering is a perfect technique for comprehending the 3D reality of the camera itself. But for whom are these books designed? The authors state that it is aimed at 'the beginner, competent amateur or expert' and as such should find a natural home in the camera section of large book shops, yet whenever I have seen it, it is placed in the children's pop-up section. Once again there seems to be a censorship at work here, disclaiming the status of books which deviate from the norm, however illuminating they are. The only time I have seen a pop-up book in the adult section of a book shop was a few years ago when one appeared satirising Victorian morals. By pulling a lever, the reader could make fashionable women of the period lift their dresses to reveal frilly underwear. It seems then that 3D books are acceptable to adults providing the subject matter is 'naughty' or trivialised in some way.

Like so many other aspects of the 3D book, the pop-up and movable book genre needs so much more study than has yet been afforded it, particularly where its role in education is concerned. But while the publishing industry classifies them as 'novelty books', and the bookshops sell them as such, it is not surprising that those concerned with pupils' learning see

them in much the same way.

However, the genre of the pop-up and movable book is not my concern here, important though they are, my concern is those 3D books which explore paper in very different ways. Of course there are wonderfully innovative children's authors and illustrators like John Burningham and Tony Ross; nevertheless the binding, structure and pagination of their books is traditional; it is the surface imagery of the page which holds their originality. The books to which I am referring are 'structurally' innovative. No doubt someone, sometime, will classify them into, say, ten main headings, with at least another ten sub-divisions producing over a hundred different 3D concepts. And that list will be out of date by the time the book is published! Whatever their aesthetic and inventive merits, the question most worth asking will be: do these books help children to learn about the ever-changing languages of communication?

On one level they entertain. Children zoom in on them, and as many parents have found to their cost, demolish them in a remarkably short period of time from overuse. Everywhere I go teachers say to me with enthusiasm, 'Have you seen . . .?', referring to some new multi-dimensional picture book. This is all good news for the publishers, who, even in times of recession generally do well in this, one of their more lucrative markets. The more spectacular the book, the more likely it is to sell. How many editors, I wonder, scout the BA illustration degree shows up and down the country each June, searching for potential children's book 'stars' to sign up? What new book forms are rolling through the print rollers as I write, as each children's publisher tries to upstage its rivals? Are they all just novelties, like fudge-flavoured ice cream? Can *The Jolly Postman* and *Sam's Sandwich* do something that more conventionally-conceived book forms cannot achieve?

There are those in literacy circles who would say, "Whatever it takes to turn them on to reading", in other words, whatever physical and mental contortions children have to perfect in order to 'tunnel' their way through these types of books is justified, if it enhances the dreary reading process.

Do art educators have a similar 'visual literacy' opinion about them? Do they see the paper engineered ingenuity of *Sam's Sandwich* as a step on the road to visual awareness and ultimately visual expression? I doubt it. Children's books, although essentially visual in concept and design – an environment in which an artist can let his or her imagination run riot like nowhere else – have always been the prerogative of the reading market. The artwork is there to weaken the resistance of children engaged in decoding texts. How many art education books can you name that give more than a passing reference to illustration? Until recently the literacy imperative has rendered the visual narrative of children's books almost impotent, awarding it at best a servicing role. A consequence of this is that art education – always ambiguous about the status of the book in general and illustration in particular – has distanced itself from it too, preferring to indulge in the safer zones of drawing and painting.

Books as sculpture

But there is a third level on which books like these have uses, and it is one which is barely recognised and the least understood. More especially, they introduce new ways in which books work – for books are a kind of enigmatic machine – and show us how words and images interrelate in fresh and invigorating ways to impart knowledge and enlighten perception. I am talking about the book as a multi-dimentionally-conceived object or, as I increasingly think of it, as paper architecture. To wrap concepts around what I am saying, we need to look at the ideas and artefacts which, to a greater or lesser degree, exist outside what is conventionally accepted as book forms.

Sculpture is a kind of non-functional architecture but it has never really had the status of painting in western culture. Of course Michelangelo's sculpture of David is as well known as his paintings on the Sistine Chapel ceiling, and art historians go into raptures about both, but the artists who predominate in the last few hundred years lean heavily towards the media of painting (when you see the word 'artist' don't you think immediately of a painter?). Sculpture is problematic because you have to walk around it to appreciate its form. Paintings are so much easier to absorb because, placed on a wall, they fit comfortably into the social ambience of a sitting room. Sculpture is so awkward. A painting in a frame has a certain intimacy and charm that sculpture lacks. Perhaps sculpture is too much like us – three-dimensional – and we prefer the romance of illusionist paint on canvas.

So the notion of the book as sculpture – something to be touched, and handled – is harder to feel at ease with than the concept of the book as something you look at, like a painting. Like Alice looking not *at* the mirror but what she sees *through* it, we look not at the book's form but rather at what is on the other side of the paper sculpture, the 2D artwork and text. It is not surprising therefore, that, whilst several books and exhibitions have been dedicated to the illustration and illustrators of the children's books, hardly anything has been done to celebrate the innovative three-dimensionality of the genre.

On the face of it, sculpture is non-functional, whereas the book is functional. But is a book really functional? Can you do anything with it other than decode the text and the pictures? Or is it that books make us *do* something in some active, practical way that makes them functional? Conceptually, at least, both can be seen as serving different ends while being aesthetic objects. The classic leather-bound, multi-sectioned, gold-tooled book looks good and feels good in the hand. It is a visual and tactile experience before its contents are examined and evaluated. But once a book is opened, it parts company with its concept as sculpture, for whilst one sees into the forms of wood or stone, the eye is not permitted to penetrate the material itself, only the points of the surface area on which the eye travels. One's own cognition creates, as it were, what is not seen but what is reasoned to be beneath the surface in a symbolic sense.

Conversely, architecture, which is functional, opens its organs to our inspection; indeed, it is its practical inner working, like the book, which gives it life. Just as the building is rooted in the ground beneath it, so the book is anchored to its spine. Both grow outward and upward. The classical book form, like classical architecture, is a model of symmetrical harmony. Everything radiates from the centre. Can one compare present-day book concepts and architecture in the same way? Does the high-tech Lloyds building in London have a match in book form?

To find an answer to this question one would need to examine what is on offer in our large book stores. Fiction predominates in the ground floor blocks of books in my local book store. The dust jackets on most titles proclaim that they 'break new ground in writing' and state that the author is the greatest visionary of the decade. However true or false this publicity hype is, what is noticeable by its absence is innovation in the book form itself. Whatever innovation in plot gymnastics is going on in the play of words 'on the page', the page itself, and the book which holds it, has experienced barely any change at all in the last hundred – one might even say thousand – years. Examining the other categories of books for adults, for example DIY manuals and cook books, one is aware of the growing importance attached to the visual images in them and changes in the ways pages are designed – I have more to say about this later – but this is new wine in old bottles, the bottle itself is unchanged. Metaphorically speaking, however asymmetrical and 'multi-dimensional' the text may be, the book as architecture will be as symmetrical as the eighteenth-century stately mansion. Just how important is the 3D technological structure of the book to the concepts

Experimental 3D book by Jean Berloff

of communication it holds? Why is it that only children's books have achieved liberation in this way?

Both these questions are larger than they may seem, and I am not sure that the question has been asked that often, or indeed has been seen as worth asking. Writers and publishers of fiction are not known for their visual sensibility. Paradoxically, visual sensitivity – the ability to 'see' what is happening around one with clarity and vision – a quality essential to the writer, does not usually extend to the application of that vision in anything

other than verbal expressions. But to say that the adult book form is basically unchanged since Caxton is not entirely true. There are two genres in which change is much in evidence.

Experimental books

The *livre d'artiste* movement in experimental book forms, seeded during the Dadaist twenties and thirties, and which has had a consistent if somewhat esoteric following ever since, has produced work as three-dimensional and varied as modern architecture. Perel Buchler (1986) argues that the rejection of the concept of art as object in the sixties put into the melting pot our whole conception of what art is. In this revolutionary period of ideas, the book was reappraised and became a concept worthy of artists' intelligence and therefore paradoxically an 'object' in an increasingly 'non-object' art scene. Most capital cities have at least one shop specialising in artists' books. It is perhaps something of an irony that the power of the book to communicate through accessible words and images reduces its status as an art object. It has to be elevated to the status of an icon – non-functional sculpture – before it is accepted by fine art. So whilst words and images do appear in artists' books they tend to be there as statements about such things, often iconoclastically so, rather than as a fundamental means of communication *per se*. In an attempt to make 'statements about books' – and to break us out of our complacency about this old and revered institution – book artists have dissected and transformed the physical structure of them in quite astonishing ways. No exhibition of artists' books is complete without the statutory meat cleaver sticking out of one of the exhibits, or books which have been set on fire, dynamited, drenched in oil or encased in lead.

The genre of designer book binding has always been at the more refined end of this experimental scene. Philip Smith (1982), one of the most sophisticated and highly regarded members of the creative book binding movement, says this about the book form:

'The book-binding artist's concern, like that of the artist using other media, lies in pushing back the frontiers of aesthetic experience and knowledge, . . . only centuries of arbitrary decoration . . . has blurred us to this potential in the book form. The book is taken for granted.'

For the book artist, the book transcends the conventional roles of graphic communication and throws into disarray commercially published conventions. Perhaps, as Smith says, the book has come too easily to us; like comfortable living we no longer know what it is we are experiencing. We need a jolt to make us re-evaluate our most familiar *modus operandi*.

The other book concept that breaks with the conventional code of adult published forms can be found under the aegis of advertising. Recently a friend showed me an advertising brochure which was triangular in shape. To examine its contents one had to open it up spirally, and in doing so a sculpture was made. Banks and building societies compete with each other to produce the ultimate in advertising material; no expense is spared; engineered doors, pop-ups and sections which open up three-dimensionally dance about their brochures in ingenious ways. In San Francisco I recently bought a pop-up map of the city, and I have seen a season of concert programmes which, when folded, produces a model of the concert hall. Clearly there is nothing here which is in the slightest way related to *livres d'artiste*, indeed no two genres could be more ideologically polarised. Yet they both probe at the conventional idea of the hinged and regular book form. Both are freed from the constraints imposed by the historical literature-oriented book ideal that has held civilisation in a vice for over a thousand years. When this occurs anything can happen, perhaps sometimes more than the genre can take, for authors and the reading public do not take kindly to having their habits changed.

Now where do children's books fit into all of this? It is difficult to see any link between them and *livres d'artiste*. There is a total lack of aesthetic snobbery in children's books, no art or anti-art statements to be made. Of course *The Jolly Postman* does make the book form which holds the novel look *passé*, but with children's books on another conceptual level to the adult book, nobody really sees it.

When one turns to advertising publishing one can discern, on the surface at least, a clearer link with the architectural nature of books for children. Because advertising is not normally regarded as an art – a branch of western culture – but as 'design', using the techniques of fine art to its own ends, what it loses in status it gains in freedom of invention. Children's books are seen as being in the same peripheral territory, not real literature, but a kind of pre-literature literature: thus, anything is permissible. It is no accident that as 'books for children' slide into the 'books for adolescents' category they become less experimental in architectural form. This unwritten law states that as children are led into the ways of cerebral activity (adulthood) all that is worth communicating is done by words alone, with the *ad hoc* assistance of visual support systems along the way. Fiction intended for the secondary school pupil is architectural only in the classical outer shell of the book, the splash of colour of the title and 'selling' artwork. Visually communicated information, so much part of children's picture books, often occupying more space on the page than text, 'develops' (regresses?) into the children's novel, with an illustration every ten pages or so, eventually reaching the adolescent/adult novel stage minus any illustrations whatsoever.

Now to discuss illustration is to enter into another domain of the book concept beyond my scope here; nevertheless the notion of the book as architecture is meaningless without it; just as it is meaningless to discuss the structure of medieval cathedrals without reference to that which is expressed on flat surfaces like stained glass and wall paintings. Architecture embraces not only structural principles of design, but everything that manifests the construction, down to surface decoration. It is worth turning here to that quintessential writer on architecture, Nikolaus Pevsner. 'Aesthetic sensations' may be caused by a building in three ways. (*a*) by surface design, e.g. proportions of windows or the leaf and fruit garlands of a Wren porch, (*b*) the exterior of a building, e.g. the effect of a dome, and (*c*) the interior, e.g. the stately movement of a baroque staircase. The first of these, two-dimensional, is the painter's way. The second is three-dimensional and is the sculptor's way. The third is more the architect's way.

> What distinguishes architecture from painting and sculpture is its spatial quality. In this, and only this, no other artist can emulate the architect.
>
> (Pevsner, 1943)

In this definition of architecture one could see the cover design and painted salad in *Sam's Sandwich* as 'the painter's way'; the shaped sandwich form as 'the sculptor's way'; and the movable interior of the sandwich as 'the architect's way'. What is particularly interesting about this notion of the book as architecture is that three different modes of conceiving form are contained in the one paper object. Existing in a 2D 'text book' world of communication we fail to be influenced, overtly at least, by other ways of seeing.

Children's books and advertising have one thing in common: no restrictions are placed upon them by aesthetic canons; they are free to communicate using whatever visual techniques are at their disposal.

Books for a new millennium

So it is to children's books and advertising publicity that we must turn for a key to architectural concepts in paper form. But there is a distinction between them. The advertising industry, although freed from the restraints of the adult book, is restricted by the real or apparent demands of their clients. Innovation in advertising design is solely a consumer wooing exercise. The shock of the inventive or novel way of folding paper is there to hold an audience just long enough to get them into the advertising copy. Consequently, creative development and depth is minimal. Marketing analysts know that their audience is predominantly conservative and will tolerate innovation only up to a point. That is the tragedy of the advertising designer; whereas the

children's book creator has almost no restrictions on the range of his or her inventiveness. The child, as consumer, is as liberal as it is possible to be.

But there is another reason why the third dimension has captured the imagination of advertising and the makers of children's books. Anyone who not only looks *at* the best of advertising illustration but *into* it, cannot fail to be impressed by the advanced skills of draughtsmanship it evidences. The pressure upon design illustrators to 'hold the eye' of the consumer a second or two longer in their advertisements than a rival, has driven them to near distraction in the race to discover something new in imagery and the use of materials. Every technique has been exploited from action painting to photographic realism, the methods of the impressionists and surrealists to pop art and op art. Sooner or later the two dimensional genre was sure to run out of steam; after all, there is only so much you can do with a pen, or paintbrush, ink, pencil, crayon or paint. To find a new field, an unexplored territory, the illustrator/designer searched the aesthetic horizon for a virgin, unexploited language. It was only a matter of time before the third dimension would be seen as the illustrator's saviour. In *3-Dimensional Illustration* (Dimensional Illustrators, 1991) winners of the first annual dimensional illustrators awards show their work, setting the seal on the international advertising of the nineties. They use all the materials and techniques of the sculptor – wood, clay, plastic, textiles and paper. Of course, the presentation of their 3D creations is in 2D photographic form. As I have said, the problem of the sculptural form, and why it has always had a low profile in fine art, is because they are such awkward things to move about and display. The flat, photographic image gives the onlooker the illusion of experiencing 3D reality without any of the spatial problems associated with the form itself.

Now children's book creators have gone one step further than this. Like those in the advertising field they have felt the need to explore visual techniques to the fullest and use virtually every traditional and modern mark-making material. They have also moved into the 3D zone in producing imagery which is sculptural in origin, but 2D in photographic presentation. Two good examples of this are *Where the Forest Meets the Sea* (Baker, 1987) and *The Paper Crane* (Bang, 1985). In the former, the rainforest is simulated in astonishing low relief photo-realism. The sand on the beach is clearly made from real sand with real footmark indentations on it. In the latter book, the shadows which are cast from low relief paper sculpture give the impression that the illustrations are far more three-dimensional than they really are. I fancy we are in for a lot more of this kind of 3D artwork in children's books in the future. But as *Sam's Sandwich* exemplifies, it is not the 2D presentation of 3D reality that children are experiencing in so many of their books but the real, spatial thing itself.

Advertising also presents the quasi-book form in 3D, as in the case of those window displays advertising mortgages, and the pop-up maps to which I have already referred; but they are conceptually simplistic in comparision with the multi-dimensional layering of 'architectural' children's books. Advertisers are imprisoned by having to reduce everything to what can be assimilated by a few seconds' scansion whereas the child 'dwells' in a book, is 'lost' in the pages, and will spend hours lifting flaps, opening envelopes and finding answers to the riddles hidden under pop-ups.

So the 3D children's books of today are unequalled in the way they are pushing forwards the concept of what a book 'is'. But is this architectural concept really that significant in the way children acquire literacy and visual communication skills, and ultimately use them, reciprocally, in their own writing, illustration and design? I wonder if, in those frozen scriptoria where the early codices were produced, monks ever asked themselves if this book thing would catch on. Did Gutenberg think that his movable type was irreplaceable? Could William Morris have contemplated the colour processing techniques of today or DTP? The book, never standing still, is now entering its next great transformation – the architecturally conceived book! No one can argue convincingly that this new era made possible by children is mere trivia. But it is also a time for assessment. For every innovative book there are a hundred or more which parasitically feed off it in some way in order to make a quick buck. We must be diligent in critically appraising the new architecturally conceived books and learn a new language of scansion and analysis in order to evaluate their worth.

For as parents and teachers – like our children and pupils – it is a time for re-experiencing the tactility of shaped paper in the book form, a much older, even primordial experience which our cerebrally dominated curriculum hides from view. So together we must take what is very old and very new and face the communication demands of our advanced society head on.

So much of what has been taken for granted about the book – as a passive holding device for words – needs to be cleared away from its form, so that in education its transformative magnitude can begin to be absorbed into the way we all learn. Our children will need training in new decoding skills; for the ones we presently train them in are woefully inadequate. The reader is required to make a journey, not metaphorically, as has been the case in the past, but actually, through doors in pages, along corridors in pull-out sections, through turning wheels, to discover important pieces of information. Subtleties of meaning can only be found by opening folders and maps, extracting books within books which themselves are in containers, and which relate to other, more complex ideas later in the book. And not only do these new processes exist solely in the picture book genre; look through the information and science shelves of the children's section in book shops and you will see that there too a transformation is taking place with, for example, science experiments which take place *in* the book itself.

No other domain of publishing, at any time in its history has established such new possibilities for the book than the children's publishing of our time. They are light years ahead of anything available for adults. The implications for the way children learn to communicate graphically are enormous. It is time that teachers and educators got to work on it.

② *Folded words and images*

'Inside my book there are all kinds of things
you can take out,' said Rachel.
To which Hannah replied,
'Yes, and put back in again'.

Vanessa, a nursery teacher, describes how she
introduced the making of books to her four-year-
olds by giving them a basic, blank, concertina
book.

'There was very little adult intervention. I just let the
children explore the books and use them as they
wished. Some children stretched out the concertina so
that they could write across the whole length at once;
others turned the pages. It was a very interesting
exercise, as it enabled me to see which children were
using it as a book, i.e. turning a page at a time. It also
allowed me to assess which children were distinguishing
'writing' from pictures, and which ones had a story or
purpose in mind as they were writing.'

*'The register' (12 × 9)
by Claire (4)*

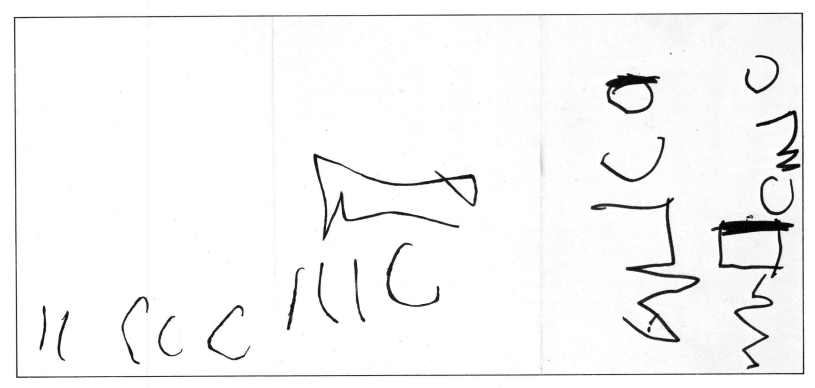

Claire planned her book as a class register. She drew her face on the front and name on the back. On the two middle pages she marked the lines (dashes and circles) as she saw Vanessa do each morning. At this emergent stage of symbol making Claire has observed one manifestation of the book concept, a system for checking school attendance, and created one like it. Already she is aware that the book has a cover and that, in a sense, it is an unimportant part of the book's function. Once inside the book, she demonstrates her knowledge of different kinds of marks, that they are processed in lines and that they have a specific meaning.

Coming forward six or so years, we have the first double page of Sarah's autobiography. It is worth analysing how she has organised the spread. The introduction in two lively sentences entices the reader by promising the revelation of 'the most memorable moments of her life'. Next,

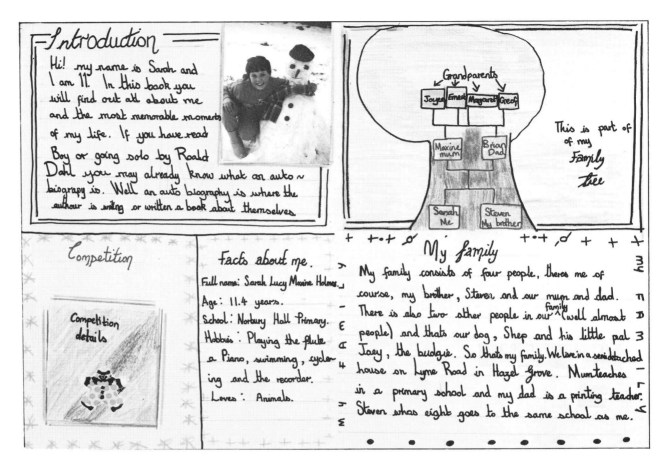

'Me' (15 × 22)
by Sarah (10/11)

referring to one of the most revered story writers of them all, Roald Dahl, she defines in two brief sentences what an autobiography is. An accompanying photograph shows us the author with a snowman. The bottom half of the page is in two parts. First, a wallet holding 'competition details', inside which is a removable strip listing the rules for entering the competition and a description of the competition itself. The other half records factual details about Sarah, like her full name and hobbies. The other top half of the spread illustrates her family tree in diagrammatic form; and in the remaining half page she describes her family, pets and parents' occupations. On the face of it, this spread appears to be a carefully written and designed piece of work. It falls on the eyes easily, we make assumptions about its worth without really having to adopt an appraisal system. It looks 'good', although not exceptional, for a child at this age.

But what is 'good' about it? To find satisfaction in the sentence structuring, compositional form, and handwriting style can only account for some of its goodness. In fact what is happening on the page here is of enormous complexity. On one level, Sarah has arranged the spread as one might design the interior of a room, by providing harmony through shape and texture in an asymmetrical fashion. The balance of words with illustration is a basic ABABAB form – text alternating with visual material. To be more precise, to avoid repetition the pattern is AB BA BA.– so text–visual, is followed by visual–text, and then visual–text again. There is also variety in the proportions of the image blocks. The visuals on the

Diagram showing distribution of words and visuals on spread

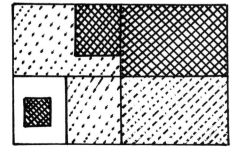

Design reduced to basic arrangement of forms

first page are roughly the same size, but as the text in the top half relates to the photograph it has been allowed to wrap itself under the image. The bottom 'competition details' visual, being conceptually independent from the textual copy, stands detached from it. The page grid, basically arranged in quarters, contrasts with the facing page, which is simply divided into two halves, horizontally.

This variety in the visual patterning of the spread not only gives clear locations for those pieces of information the book artist has decided to include, but also takes into account the psychology of scansion. The eye needs variety and things to 'hold its interest'. Like us, it gets easily bored. It needs these moments of contrast and rest in any decoding task. Margins and gaps between paragraphs are all part of the eye's need to pause and take stock. When moving from text to picture, like the photo of Sarah and the snowman, one switches from a *cognitive-verbal* mood to one of *visual-analytical* scansion. We take note of the clothes she is wearing, the fact that although there is snow on the ground the sun is shining, and we assume that the author has decorated the snowman with facial features and hat herself. It is a moment of reflection, of recognising what one is looking at, and identifying what we are being told through the image. Contrastingly, the next image, also visual, is in a purely decorative, 'distractive' mood because we realise that it 'contains' a novelty, and we are seduced by the wrapper. The kinesthetic activity of removing the competition details is another 'holding device'; even at this early stage of the book we are not being permitted to become bored for a second. The third visual image – the family tree – is larger than the others because it carries diagrammatic information which needs space, but even here a tree has been drawn around the chart to take the sting out of the decoding process.

On another level, one can analyse the use of writing styles and how these interact with the visual forms. We have already seen how the first few sentences are both inviting and informative. Even the description of the autobiographical concept is made compelling by referring to a well

known author. In the lower half of the page the competition rules are clearly laid out under three headings, and the 'Facts about me' section uses a similar, yet different system, that of a conventional form-filling 'list' kind. The family tree diagram uses names in boxes joined by a linear framework defining the relationship of those recorded. The last piece of writing is descriptive in style and developmental in character. Notice how well Sarah has planned the areas of text to fit the grid. The last word of the final sentence in 'The Introduction' and 'My Family' arrive exactly where the line finishes. This is an accomplishment, for it is far easier to fit a drawing into a space than a piece of writing, because in the latter every centimetre has its designation – a word, or a space between them.

Now how much of this design sense both in 'copy' writing, visual forms and the relationship between them, was consciously applied by Sarah? We learn from the text that both her parents are teachers (her father a teacher of printing!) so maybe she has an advantage over most children. Sarah is one of a group of children in a Stockport school that I 'commission' to make books on a regular basis, and this autobiography was one of the topics I gave them. I had thought of interviewing her about the genesis and structure of her study but wasn't sure if it was that important to know. If her father helped her to assemble it, we can only learn from his professional expertise, and perhaps he should be writing this book, not me; and if she did the whole thing from intuitive intelligence – her experience of how ideas are communicated through books somehow reciprocally assimilated by her – then little could be

divulged through questioning. I prefer, like looking at a Van Gogh, to ask the question: What does this object tell me about the person who made it? And then to use that information in formulating ideas about how it influences the way others might be guided into learning through something similar. For if such things are significant to successful communication, then they are of relevance to the curriculum, and we must learn the grammar of it if we are to teach it well.

Of course, there are some weaknesses in her book. Grammatical error, insufficiently spaced margins, and a photograph which is too high on the page, are three of them. But whatever the source of her book-processing skills, she has assembled here, on one double page, over twenty different graphic communication techniques. And none of those techniques belongs exclusively to the autobiographical genre. Indeed, there can hardly be a curriculum subject which, in published book form at least, does not use all of them, and a great many more besides.

But how important is it for children to have these skills? Isn't it, after all, just an attractive embellishment of graphic communication in general, and not the essence of it? And besides, how significant is 'graphic' communication anyway?

A new language of communication

Our day-to-day experience of well-designed reading material like magazines and reference books blinds us to what it is we are looking at. Does any one of us consciously break down the page we are reading into a design concept and ask questions like: Is that photograph too large for the page, and is it placed in the right position? Does the accompanying caption really tell me something that isn't patently obvious in the photograph, and is that block of text in the best font and size for the area of the page it lies on? Professional graphic designers are incapable of just 'enjoying' a magazine or book page, as you or I might do, because all they can see there is the designer's communication concept and how successful he or she has been at it. For them, the clarity and appropriateness of graphic communication strategies are inseparable from that which is being communicated in a linguistic or visual form, in fact they would argue that some kind of cerebral, non-visually-conceived communication is a contradiction in terms. There is just good and bad visual communication. It may not do too much for our self-confidence to be made aware that most of what we write – letters, captions, labels, notices, annotated diagrams – are just bad forms of visually-communicated information. Yet how many of us think about such things beyond the statutory need to apologise for our handwriting? Design is 'out there' in some irreproachable terrain like the writing of symphonies and epic poetry.

However, the most basic visual communication of all, writing a sentence, requires sophisticated design skills not only in the way we shape letters but the spaces between them and between words. Whether we are aware of this or not, or imagine ourselves to be visually inept, design impinges upon every aspect of how we communicate graphically to others. The computer has brought

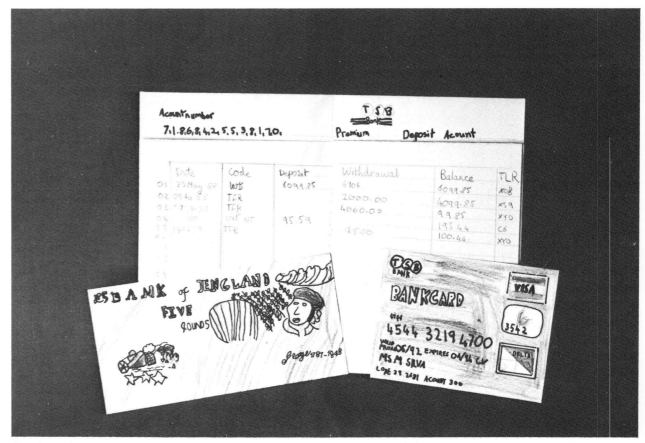

'Banking' (23 × 16) Emma and Mariana (8/9)

this into sharp focus. Take design away from our most fundamental communication methods and advanced western society would collapse.

When Claire simulated the class register in her nursery she was taking the first step down the road of learning which is mountain-high with different kinds of symbolic systems. Gradually she will add to her repertoire of forms, and if she is lucky enough to have teachers like Vanessa throughout her schooling, the forms through which she synthesises her growing knowledge will be in the book form, because that is where her experience will come from too.

Look at Emma and Mariana's banking project (above and page 30). Age-wise, they are between Claire and Sarah. Already they are discovering refined and polished ways of communicating information. They have learnt that using cheques is a technique enabling those with money in a bank to withdraw it. They have also understood that a bank card is used in conjunction with a cheque when making purchases, and that a paying-in slip is used when you put money into the bank. Later they will learn to understand what things like current accounts are and that the various sequences of numbers on all these objects have specific meanings and uses.

Now they could have discovered this information by consulting a book on the subject and 'writing about it' in an exercise book. But every sensitive teacher knows from experience that the direct process of creative involvement is the most pragmatic way of learning anything. By Emma and Mariana collaboratively using a real cheque as a guide to simulating one of their own, they have learnt what Leonardo discovered 500 years ago: 'knowledge through drawing' or more precisely, knowledge through drawing design.

The design skills they are learning in placing coded marks on paper will set them on the road to communication. The placing of words and mathematical symbols in a specific pattern, and knowing why you have done it, is as much a 'grammar' as the linguistic one is. The holding form for all that research and sequencing of data – the book – will have made the whole enterprise that much more easy to grasp.

Of the mountains of books on literacy and English teaching for which additional shelving systems had to be installed in college libraries during the eighties, one – a book so small that it was impossible to give even a slender spine to it – probably said more that was new and fresh about children's aquisition of literacy than any other. This book was Margaret Meek's (1988) *How Texts Teach What Readers Learn*, published by the appropriately named Thimble Press. In it, a discussion of what a child actually experiences when confronted with a typical children's picture book – the galaxy of forms, both visual and linguistic, and the experience that is brought to the scanning task – gave a new way of thinking not only to the way children learn to read and write, but to the way in which they engage in the whole visual dimension of learning. And if this is a realistic definition of what a young child's arrival into a literate community should be – that a picture book contains a multi-layering of communication systems – should it not be a definition of what they should be writing, and the form of that writing too?

The uses of minimalism

If one short sentence in a TV commercial costs thousands of pounds for the air-time it takes to say it, then words have become the most precious icons of our time. In every part of our lives we are encouraged to be economical. If it is true that to eat less is to be healthier, could it not also be true that to use fewer words is a healthier way to communicate? Compare any magazine published thirty years ago to those of today. Of the many stylistic differences apparent on the pages (and ignoring developments in printing techniques) what stands out most is the difference in design concepts. In earlier magazines words predominate the page spread, text and images tend to stand apart and there is little adventurousness in the way that both forms coexist on the page. They are somewhat like the adult novel of today, except that they have pictures; just as the magazine of today is like a children's picture book of today in terms of what is new.

One senses in present-day magazines with a high profile like *Marie Claire*, for example, that typography and visual imagery have been liberated in a way that the typographical experimentalists before the war, like Reichert and Dieter Rot, must have dreamt would happen in publishing one day. The magazine exists outside the rule-orientated literature hierarchy. Its ephemeral nature gives it low status; books you keep; magazines you throw away. Journalists are looked down on by the literati as the lowest species of literate life there is. This is the journalists' tragedy, but it is also the source of their freedom to innovate. It releases journalists and the whole magazine design machinery to experiment with the page concept, and consequently makes the best of them some of the most exciting pioneers in the word communication genre.

Over the years book format and length has changed considerably. In Victorian times some popular books stretched to two or sometimes three volumes. Even books by such famous writers as Charles Dickens or Thomas Hardy nearly always contained five or six hundred pages of very small print. Today, on the other hand, people generally prefer much shorter stories. With so many other forms of entertainment available, such as radio and television, most people do not want to spend days, or even weeks, reading a book. The novels of Graham Greene, for example, who is regarded as one of the finest writers of this century, are rarely more than 300 pages long (Wilkins, 1982).

In all forms of communication, sentences and paragraphs are tending to get shorter. In magazines, like the advertising media, just one word is sometimes used to symbolise a whole concept. In addition to this, the growing use of visual forms, from line drawings to photographs, and – like children's book illustrations – a great deal of graphic and colour exploration, has made them more 'visual' than ever. It is not just the artwork which exploits colour but the text and captions too. Not unlike the experiments of Marinetti and the futurist movement of seventy years ago, words now dance about the page, and it is increasingly difficult to categorically determine, in some cases, which part of the page is for text and which illustration! It is as if the great divide between word and image, supported by the literary hierarchy for so long, has at last been demolished.

Of course it is no such thing – few writers are aware of how artwork can often define more clearly what they are trying to say with words – but at least one can feel a strong wind of change in the influence of the graphic communications industry on all forms of writing. Advertising, so much a part of the substance of magazines, has perhaps been the main influence of this interrelation of forms, and from where art editors have taken their inspiration. But while advertising has mastered the language of minimalism, it has also been imprisoned by it. As has been argued, the politics of advertising proscribes development.

Is there a link between the changing patterns of how the communications industries use words and images, and what should be happening to the way children learn?

It is appropriate that a magazine with a high fashion profile like the award-winning *Marie Claire* should conceive just about every page as a design challenge. One is tempted to analyse in depth the

Extract from **Marie Claire**
July, 1992

page above and compare it to Sarah's autobiography. At a glance they may seem far apart, yet on closer inspection they are remarkably similar. Both use short written statements to introduce different aspects of the same theme. On the fashion page the areas of type (it would be incorrect to call them 'blocks' for not one of them has parallel vertical edges) alternate plain and **bold** and are arranged, curvaceously, to harmonise with the forms of the artwork. Sarah's introductory text relates to her illustration in this way, but she doesn't have the DTP technology at her fingertips to 'contour' the rest of the text. Both interrelate text and visuals. The fashion illustrations use artwork to define a design concept, and photographs to show made-up garments. Horizontal sunglasses and case balance vertical standing figures, and the casually arranged jewellery (in black and white to contrast with the colour images) acts as a relaxing motif against all the other pieces of tightly packed, minimalist copy. In Sarah's book, the competition details are a light relief like the jewellery in the magazine. She too uses a graphic diagram (the family tree) to convey a concept. The photograph of her and the snowman – like the modelled bathing costume – shows us the reality of the subject as only a photograph can.

This comparison doesn't stop there; one could compare how essential ideas are expressed through carefully chosen words, and the psychological organisation of colour, but more importantly it illustrates how a primary-age child can communicate through the same highly sophisticated and masterly techniques as a professional. For her to have provided the reader

with the same information contained on the spread, but using solely verbal descriptions, would have taken her not two, but as many as five or six pages. And even then, assuming that she has acquired the ability to handle words confidently, would those six pages have communicated the same information with as much clarity as the multiple imagery of the double-page spread? I think it unlikely.

Of course, it is not just information she is conveying. Like the magazine designer she is engrossed with the psychology of the reader. If the reader gets bored with either monotonous lines of print, or having to absorb too much information in a small space, he or she will turn off from the decoding process. The casually arranged jewellery and the competition details are as much part of the psychology of authorship as the meatier substance of the page, and require as much imaginative competence to blend it into one spatial design. Sarah is not only writing for an audience, she has, albeit unconsciously, done her market research on the social psychology of that audience as well.

New uses for old works

The page from *Marie Claire* exemplifies what can be seen in the galaxy of magazines, on every subject from angling to collecting antiques, filling whole walls, from floor to ceiling, in newsagents. It is an international language crossing all national and cultural boundaries. Go through the *Radio Times* and see the art of minimalism at its most professional and profound! Moreover, in even more developmental ways, this 'multi-layering' of

visually communicated information can be experienced in many of the sixty-thousand-odd new book titles which appear in the UK each year. School text books on subjects like science, geography and the environment would fail the children they serve without this cross-coding of symbolic devices. Consult the striking Dorling Kindersley reference books like the award-winning *Inside the Whale* by Ted Dewan (1992), and *The Way Things Work* by that master of children's information book design, David Macaulay (1988), and you will see just how sharply defined concepts can be expressed in only one page of carefully constructed words and images.

But isn't there a danger with this new minimalism being taught to children? If reading literature transports them to another world which can hold them for hours or days on end, isn't it just as justifiable that they should have the same kind of freedom to write at length? Doesn't 'developmental writing' mean being able to expand concepts at length? And if the pupil must stop to ask the question: 'Would it be better to draw this idea rather than write about it', wouldn't that break the flow of thought?

There must always be a place in the curriculum for unchallenged modes of authorship. There have been times in my life when to write and write and write, almost without pause, was an intellectual and emotional necessity growing out of an important experience. Minimalism could have done nothing for that spontaneous need. But similarly, that most ancient minimalist expression of them all – poetry – has come to me like a gift when feelings could only be matched by ten or fifteen endlessly redrafted words. Aren't the best writers those who bring the refining influence of poetry to bear on their work? Isn't 'crafted' writing an expression which is simultaneously simple (but not simplistic) and complex, or to put it another way: the complexity is expressed through simplicity? George Bernard Shaw summed up the refining process when, at the end of a letter to a friend he apologised for it being so long because he didn't have time to write a short one.

In most teaching situations we want our children to write not more, but less – quality, not quantity. How often do we, knocking out all the conjunctive 'ands', and repetitions from a pupil's story, reduce a page of text to a couple of sentences? The popularity of haiku is not just due to our fascination with the mystic East, but because it gives us a precise structure in which to create a monumental statement in a miniscule poem. Poets and copy editors – although culturally polarised – know, like no others, that small is beautiful. The art of refining concentrates the mind wonderfully. There is nothing minimal about the concept of quality minimalism. It just seems that way.

How words and art relate, and whether or not, combined, they assist knowledge and understanding or slow the whole thing down, needs far more in-depth research and debate, but when drawings, diagrams and photographs can show certain processes and physical elements with a factual clarity unavailable to the user of words, the absence of these skills can only be detrimental to the 'seeker after truth'.

Whether there is a 'minimalistic' language of visual art, or how one might use it if it exists, is another question without an easily identified answer; for whilst linguistic language has been categorised at length, art language has never been systematically analysed, at least not in the way children process drawing in order to learn across the curriculum. We can sense in an apparently improvised drawing by Matisse that three well-placed flowing lines can express the female form more accurately than those painfully overpainted nudes of the eighteenth century, but is it a 'language' which can be taught, and is it transferable to other modes of drawing?

So where does the 'book searching for authors' fit into the quest for minimalism and the multi-layered page?

The magic of the book form is that however much you think you have to say, it will almost certainly have some sound advice to give you. The first double page of Sarah's self-portrait 'told' her how to use its space, but only because she was receptive to what it had to say, although she may not have been aware of it. And she had behind her all that day-to-day experience of environmental print and TV giving her messages adaptable to her own need to communicate.

All over Britain, on my travels, I see books made by children which have merits of one kind or another, but where they fall down most is that the author *did not sufficiently listen to the page*. This is because, ever since books were first used in classrooms, no connection has ever been seriously made between how the page communicates information, and how the pupil then communicates what he or she has learnt *through*

the book, *in* a book. The ideas implicit in the text and illustrations in the book have been digested, but not the *manner* of communication. It is as if what one is looking at is hidden from view, and what one sees is a preconceived idea of what should be there. Nothing else could contain the vast range of stories, fashion and health features, information about new novels, films and music and a diversity of advertising material than succinct magazine forms like *Marie Claire*. The host of letter forms in *The Jolly Postman* could not have been conceived without the dynamism of the book form to plan and organise it on behalf of the Ahlbergs. Books have learnt so much over the years about the dissemination of information. Far more than you or I could formulate by ourselves.

A book of our time

The Jolly Postman, perhaps more than any other item of children's publishing of its time brought into focus the enigma of the book. By being a book which didn't behave like one, and didn't behave like anything else either, it held our curiosity. It helped to liberate what an author/illustrator could invent and still call a book. Although some felt that it was not as good as its predecessor, *The Jolly Christmas Postman* went even further in what a book could 'contain' and still be classified as one. How far these architectural books can be taken remains to be seen. But *The Jolly Postman* did more than this; it innovated another way for a story to be told.

One of the reasons why there is such an upheaval today in the teaching of English is because some have held it up to the uses of language in the 'outside world' and found it wanting. Whether or not one accepts this criticism is beside the point: what is for certain is that children need to acquire a greater range of communication skills than ever before to make sense of both the world around them, and what they have to contribute to its survival. Trends in English teaching have emphasised what has come to be known as 'non-narrational' and/or 'non-chronological' modes of writing because, it is held, they *belong* to the work-a-day environment outside the cloistered walls of educational establishments. These terms are vague, and have become umbrella terms for anything which is other than narrational and *chronological*, but as these terms are far from clear too, perhaps the confusion is not surprising. What *The Jolly Postman* shows is how these so-called narrational and non-narrational forms can coexist organically *in* the book.

To take just one of the book's sections beginning with a rhyming narrative:

Off went the Postman
    Toodle-oo!
In his uniform of postal blue
    To a gingerbread cottage –
And garage too!

With a letter for the Wicked Witch.

This leads directly to the envelope marked:

OPEN NOW – DON'T DELAY
This could be your lucky day!

followed by:

FREE Witch Watch with every order

Inside the envelope is another joke, this time at the expense of advertising junk mail; a sheet listing hilarious merchandise, like 'Little Boy Pie Mix' and 'Cup and Sorcerer Tea Service'. The next, and final page of this section completes the Witch episode with rhyming narrative again:

So the Witch read the letter
    With a cackle of glee
While the Postman read the paper
    But *left* his tea. (It was green!)

Above the text is an illustration of the witch reading the contents of the envelope while the postman sits reading a newspaper – 'Mirror Mirror'. The witch's cat is doing the washing up at the sink and a bat hangs from a linen horse.

I haven't counted them, but there must be ten to fifteen different classifications of writing forms here. As in the operations of the 'real world', this fantasy ambience of the story-teller meanders with ease through narrative and non-narrative forms. The section begins and ends with the same narrative form, but between them are sandwiched a whole range of advertising one-liners and instructions. Additionally, visual forms illuminate the text: for example the drawing of the toadstool lamp in the *Deadly Lampshades* advertisement highlights the play on words. In the illustration accompanying the concluding narrative, we see on the newspaper the postman is reading references to other characters in the story.

It might be stretching it a bit to say that *The Jolly Postman*, *Marie Claire* magazine, and Sarah's autobiography are basically the same structurally, but they do share many things in common; the

most significant being the inter-connection of different styles of writing and visual communication. They do it in different ways, over different formal arrangements of pages, and their objectives are different too. What they all exemplify is the multiplicity of symbolic communication systems which characterise the diversity of our times, not just in writing but in the whole nature of social intercourse.

The *Jolly Postman* books simultaneously celebrate and satirise our western market economy. The stupidity of so much advertising copy is pin-pointed; we are encouraged to laugh at the way we are taken in by it all. There may well be a political message here, whether or not it is intentional is open to debate, but the humour embedded in the whole format invites readers to draw their own conclusions about the ethics of the consumer society unobtrusively.

On another level, the books draw attention to the diversity of forms contained within them because they are not *real* envelopes and letters, but *interpretations* of real objects. Even very young readers know that. The envelope caption 'Open Now – Don't Delay . . .' is in Janet Ahlberg's *drawn* letters. They are slightly imperfect, which is the charm and hallmark of the non-mechanically produced image. Just as Jasper Johns' famous 'stars and stripes' paintings of the sixties pop-art movement made their audience suddenly aware of the American flag as an object, so *The Jolly Postman*'s printed ephemera jolt the reader into contemplating not what commercial mail is about, but what it *is* as object. It is a paradox of cognition that in order to perceive something familiar – to see it with a sharpened vision – one must invariably change its appearance in some way. The 'Open Now' caption, like so many junk mail envelopes, uses the technique of the diagonal orientation. We are used to reading in horizontal lines; to place them at an angle displaces the scanning process; but it is that reorientation of the hand and eye that emphasises the image. (Next time you scan a sheet of junk mail notice how often the designer is forcing the eye into changes of this kind in order to keep it alert while all those selling lines are being driven in!)

When children 'read' *The Jolly Postman* they are being introduced to many of the subtle techniques of the communications industry without being necessarily aware of it, and in a highly light-hearted way. Humour is the greatest educator.

The politics of communication

English teaching is subject to polarisation. There is the English as high art or popular culture debate. Another, similar, argument holds that the traditional *literary concept* – novel, poetry and the essay – symbolises the zenith of the subject. At the other extreme is the more recent, politically inspired, *functional concept* which argues that English is only meaningful in terms of the uses to which it can be put. In this second notion the ability to write non-chronological advertising copy is of greater significance than the skill required to pen a well written story or poem. It follows, in that line of thinking, that those who only teach narrative, descriptive and critical writing are 'not providing children with life skills'. Yet, ironically

when scripts from popular TV soap operas are included in the English curriculum teachers are accused of lowering standards. Could any form of communication reflect 'real life' more than the skills needed by the authors of situation comedy and TV commercial jingles, producing such huge financial success? Teachers will be well aware of the conceptual and political battleground on which these arguments are fought, *ad infinitum*, in the conference halls and the press.

But the truth of the matter – so vividly illustrated in *The Jolly Postman*, *Marie Claire*, Sarah's autobiography and, I hope, the rest of the children's work in this book – is that the wholeness and richness of our lives need *all* of these aspects of what the linguistic and visual languages of evolving civilisation has to offer. I would not wish to censor advertising copy skills from the curriculum, whatever views I hold about its general level of banality in published material. But a gifted copy writer can slice me in half with a palm-full of words expressing the plight of Ethiopia. I assume that most professional copy writers have an English/humanities honours degree background. Without immersion into great writing and the skills of criticism, they would never have acquired the facility with creative language that is the bedrock of their craft at its best. Children who only learn to write advertising copy would soon become brain-dead. To come up with an imaginative and original six-word advertising slogan comes from years of hard graft at the linguistic work bench. The apparently light-hearted illustration sketches of Janet Ahlberg in *The Jolly Postman* similarly conceal the years of

practice that make such dexterity possible. Successful minimalism in all its forms, including poetry and pen and ink drawing, is a fine art.

It is no longer acceptable to pretend that copy writing and communication design are two unrelated entities just because they are embodied in two indivisible subjects in the curriculum structure. If schooling is, in some measure preparing pupils for the world of work, that attitude simply will not do. We are entering a new linguistic epoch and new forms of graphic communication are visible all around us.

The Jolly Postman is a model of efficacy in this age of educational turmoil. As we have seen, it can be analysed within a curriculum context on many different levels from the idea of the book as architecture to the notion of non-narrative minimalism, and the role of design on cognition. It has provided the inspiration for this book – or more accurately – for the teachers and children whose work is reproduced here. *Marie Claire* magazine might seem an odd model in a book about children developing writing and graphic skills, but I choose it because it is one of the best designed magazines. If children are to accommodate the communication skills of the 'real world', then, pragmatically, what could be a better choice? My aim is to avoid a preconceived idea of what the curriculum should contain, but rather to use children's personal statements as the source of a proposed framework; to show what they have learnt, and try to define how that perceived learning addresses some of the educational objectives of our time. Of course, all kinds of gaps appear when one works in that way, but the advantage is that one avoids the mistake of assuming that educational idealism is educational fact. Only what children produce and the process of production is fact. The problems associated with so much of the National Curriculum in the UK have been due to its failure to take that truism into account.

My preferred approach is to lay all the tools and forms of visual communication on the table – and I include writing as a 'visual' mode – and like an engineer well trained in his art, try to understand what they are all capable of, and how they can be integrated into making something which is not only superbly functional but looks good too. I have been teaching long enough to know that children have an inner vision of their own and, with guidance, use the experiences of their lives to make statements of lucidity and depth.

Children sense, like William Morris knew, that beauty and function speak through each other.

Demystifying the method

I am coy about defining a book art *methodology* – such things usually turn out to be the kiss of death to their originator. Just as art can only be conceptualised in relation to what artists produce, so book art as a concept is only discernible in what book artists make. I have no idea what a planned definitive 'model' of book art would look like. If it is anything like most of the ideal models of learning foisted on teachers today by a legally binding system I am sure it would be equally disastrous.

All these books start with an idea, usually an

Four- and five-year-old pupils at work on a sandwich book

idea about the transformative charisma of paper. The sheet of paper is folded, cut and folded again until what one is holding is no longer a piece of paper but something else – the foundation of civilisation – a book.

What happens then is a kind of standing back for both teacher and pupil.

And watching and waiting.

And perhaps even leaving it for a while.

And then coming back to it again to see if anything has appeared in the book which now exists in another form: that of the imagination.

From here on the intricate machinery of the mind combines with the architectural folds of the book to communicate that which is unique.

Some notes on the work which follows

Children's work

To give a reasonably accurate indication of age, where, for example, 9/10 is given this indicates that the pupil is 'rising' 10, that is, a month or two before that age.

Size of work is given in centimetres: horizontal, first; vertical, second. This refers to the overall size of the closed book or card page, not the removable objects which may be attached to them or, where this is relevant, opened out sections.

Children do not always design their books with reproduction in mind, consequently it has been necessary, in a few cases, to add line work to make imagery visible.

Diagrams

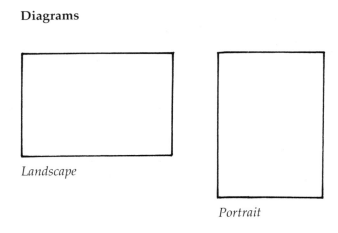

Landscape

Portrait

Most books are constructed on either landscape or portrait orientation. For technical information on construction and assembly see page 114.

Paper size

The size of the sheet of paper used to make a book determines the page dimensions when it is folded down. Obviously a book of eight pages will have smaller page sizes than one of four pages. So the size of paper you start with is significant.

Experiment with book forms on A4 (or junk mail) first and then decide the most appropriate paper size – A4 to A1 for project work. Only occasionally are measurements given in the text.

As with books in general, most of the work illustrated in this book shows left side pages as even numbered and right as odd. Thus, the first page of text is invariably numbered 2.

③ Book creating projects

① Postman books

Four-year-old Susan 'wrote' a letter to Father Christmas.
Her teacher, trying to get her to place it in an envelope said, 'Now what are you going to do with it?'
Susan responded by popping it into her teacher's blouse pocket and added, 'You're the Postman!'

Variations on a theme

It is appropriate for this journey through book forms to start with a concept inspired by *The Jolly Postman*. In *A Book of One's Own* I described one project using similar techniques to this, but in the pages which follow it is taken much further. It is also significant that the basic form from which the book is derived – the architectural base – is one of the simplest (perhaps *the* simplest) of all 'cut and fold' books (see 1, 2 and 3 opposite).

This makes a book comprising four internal pages which can be used for almost any narrative or project-based book. But to make it into 'The Postman Book' continue as follows (see 4 and 5).

The finished book is then ready for *processing*. The first text page (2) introduces the reader into the first kinesthetic activity, that of removing

whatever is contained in the tramlines (3). The slotted tramlines on the next page (4) then contain an object as a sequel to the previous one, and lead to the final textual page (5).

The tramlines replace the envelopes of *The Jolly Postman* book. This simplifies the container-making

Basic book

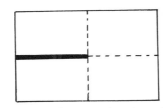

① *Crease landscape on horizontal and vertical. Cut one horizontal section.*

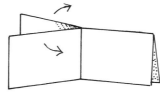

② *Fold on landscape horizontal and fold left side panels forward.*

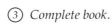

③ *Complete book.*

Basic book with tramlines

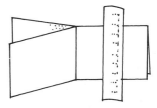

④ *Fold book pages back to 2 above. Draw line each side of steel ruler on folded panel.*

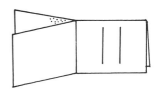

⑤ *Cut tramlines through both pieces simultaneously.*

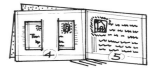

Page arrangements.

facility of the form but, as will be seen later, the envelope form reappears in another usage.

It is a truism that the simpler the form the more invention it makes possible. These simple container tramlines provide more scope for developmental cross-curricular work than almost any other structure. The reason for this is that whereas the fixed illustration is, as the word implies, a representation or interpretation of a phenomenon, that which is contained, but not attached has far greater flexibility of meaning. It is a replication of objects *in situ*, in the actual world. The object can have a front and back, can be opened, folded and rearranged into a 3D form. This facility brings the illusion of the book form into the reality of three-dimensional space and the tactile way we use objects in our daily lives.

This basic feature of having direct access to letters, cards, documents – and a host of other paper forms – introduces a new dimension into formulating and processing data as the next few examples of children's work show. Daniel D. Hade (1991) describes how he discovered that his three-year-old daughter had stuffed scribbled pieces of paper into *The Jolly Postman* envelopes. When asked about this she explained that she had written letters and was mailing them. This illustrates how significant the physical reality of paper-simulated forms are to young children.

See *'Rosie's Special Surprise Birthday'* by Tara in the colour section on page 98.

This is the first of three book projects which take parties as a theme. This one was planned by a mother for her five-year-old daughter, Tara. The technological structure is that of the basic origami book (see page 114) and not as the form described above or the rest of the books which follow. Tara was shown the six-page book and she planned a party story to go inside it including letter and other forms. The episodic text was written into the book by Tara's mother from dictation in one afternoon. Tara then drew in the illustrations, sequentially, and designed the removable objects. What is at once apparent is the awareness that illustrations are contained within rectangular boxes and illuminate aspects of the page's narration. Tara draws happy, smiling Rosie surrounded by balloons, reinforced by the speech bubble. 'What is it?' asks Rosie, in response to Candy's special present. The reader's eager anticipation is rewarded by opening the envelope on page 4 and finding a cut-out teddy bear. Tara drew her own teddy bear here and introduces her favourite video ('Spot') on page 6. The story ends with the singing of 'Happy birthday' from movable sheet music which shows that Tara is aware that both the words of a song and symbols for music can be recorded on paper. Her mother said:

> 'Tara was totally absorbed by the book as something you could hold, open, and take things out of, like a box of toys. Adding her own words and drawings, became as much a 'real' part of the book, as the removable things they were recorded on.'

See *'The Birthday Party'* by Natalie in the colour section on page 98.

This large format book (full sheet size A2) made by the teacher, enabled six-year-old Natalie to not only write and draw boldly on the pages but to have adequate space to engage in the tricky operation of inserting and removing the various documents. The book both plans and records her hypothetical birthday celebration. The cover shows her standing by her front door as an invitation to guests coming to her party. The caption to page 1, 'I say my mummy and daddy', refers to the invitation in the tramlines opposite, which is captioned, 'The inbtaysh'. The invitation, when opened out is addressed to Mummy and Daddy and states the date and time. Over the page is the caption 'The Reply', and when taken out of the tramlines and opened, the letter is from Mummy and Daddy accepting the party invitation, 'Yes I wod like to com love mummy and daddy'. The final page artwork shows Natalie with a parcel and is captioned, 'I plaied pass The parcel'.

How the project was organised

The approach with this project was for the teacher to introduce *The Jolly Postman* book to the class over several days. They took it in turn to carefully remove the letters, and the parts of the envelope – name, address, stamp, lid – were discussed. As is so often the case with favourite books, the class never seemed to tire of it, requesting for it to be 'performed' again and again. The teacher made the basic book form, the invitations (A4 folded to four A6s), and the replies (A4 folded on landscape horizontal and folded into three) for each child in the class. The party theme was discussed, the function of the tramlines demonstrated, and the content of the invitations brainstormed. Some commercially produced invitations were examined. The actual processing, however, took place in small table-group units, and so each task took about two days to be completed.

Process

1. This assisted-writing process involved deciding what was to be written (an invitation to what?), inscribing it, and designing the wording on the outside of the card. The completed card was slotted through the appropriate tramlines.

2. If there was to be a written and illustrated introduction to the card on the first inside page, 'Tomorrow is Mary's birthday party . . .', this was written in after discussing the appropriate wording.

3. The reply letter was now examined and ideas about what it should contain discussed, for example, 'When you get an invitation to a party what do you do in return?' The letter was written and inserted in the tramlines. The teacher said,

'I am sure that having a letter, attractively folded in the hand, went a long way to stimulating the children to want a write a *real* letter. We underestimate that, even at this age, they distinguish between what is real and what is not. A letter in an exercise book is not as 'real' to them as a separate, folded piece of paper.'

4. Here, pupils could choose what favourite party game they wanted to draw and caption on the last page.

5. The final task involved designing the cover with title, author's name and artwork. Classroom picture books were used here to

'The party (24 × 16) by Lucy (6)

illustrate various cover strategies, for example, title – top; illustration – centre; author – bottom.

The whole project took about two weeks to be completed without any loss of enthusiasm during this period. The teacher observed, what so many teachers of young children have stated to me, that

the kinesthetic, folding process of the book form provides children with a series of related, yet separate challenges. They see a four-page task like this as four separate pieces of work, yet having a related wholeness. Consequently, enthusiasm does not wane before the total task is complete because the 'separateness and togetherness' of it drives the thing on to a satisfactory conclusion.

Lucy's book form and theme is similar to Natalie's but at a further stage of development. The class started the project by discussing what an invitation is, and then writing about the arrival of the letter on the first, left-side page. Recording the arrival of the letter at the top of the tramlined page came next, and then writing the invitation itself. From Natalie's, 'Would you like to come to my party? . . .' comes the introduction of another communication strategy – the prescribed invitation format of 'I cannot come/I can come (please tick).'

See '**The Letter**' by Stuart in the colour section on page 98.

This book folded from A3 makes an A5 page size; an ideal scale for a pupil at this stage of development (eight years of age). The theme expressed here would be inappropriate in a larger or smaller book. There is only one set of tramlines here because the structure of the narrative only required one. How the book came into being is an interesting story. Stuart's teacher, Karen, had tried every known technique to get him to want to write. All of them had failed. Karen knew that he had one passion in life, football, so out of desperation she turned to the 'postman' book form. She spent a whole, long evening making a beautiful small envelope, inscribed it in a calligraphic style, drew in a stamp and franking. The letter she made to go inside it was even more visually delightful for she simulated the notepaper logo of Manchester United Football Club and under it wrote a letter addressed formally to Stuart inviting him to be a spectator at a match at the ground:

> 'Dear Mr Gregory
> We are pleased to inform you that your name has been selected from thousands of hopeful youngsters, and you are invited to visit Old Trafford, and meet the whole team on Saturday 3 November. Please bring along a friend or relative.
> See you soon
> Alex Ferguson'

The next morning Karen presented the unsuspecting Stuart with the letter. The reader can judge for him or herself whether the experiment worked from this beginning to his book:

> 'One Satuday morning i went down stairs to see if there was any post so there was i took it upstairs with me and got my Manchester-United kit on, and i opened it and i could not beleve it if you want to read it open the envelope.'

Whatever the weaknesses of grammar and incorrect spelling, it was Stuart's first piece of self-motivated writing. His whole attitude to writing then took a new turn. In the last two pages in the book (plus the back cover), he discusses the football stadium, a match, and the players. As Karen points out:

> 'You sometimes have to dig quite deeply to find something that inspires children. And that may be only half way to finding what motivated them to make a statement about it through words or art.'

When *The Jolly Postman* first appeared in 1986, it showed that learning letter and transactional writing skills could be one of the most exciting things one could do at school. For those children fortunate enough to make a tour through the wit and humour of the book, making connections with the lore of picture book characters as they went, developing reading and writing skills became a pleasure. And what a contrast this is to the content of those dreary lessons conducted from the blackboard showing children how to arrange a letter on a page which still goes on in less enlightened, 'back to basics' classrooms today. What the book also illustrates imaginatively is the variety of envelope forms (e.g. air mail) and styles of presentation (e.g. handwritten/typed), and the reasons for choosing one in preference to another, which is part of letter-writing knowledge.

It also raises the increasingly contentious subject of punctuation. There are some people who want to have this area of language elevated in the curriculum and who would like to have regular punctuation tests for even very young children. Other teachers see it as an inhibition to creative development. But what is the function of punctuation today?

The influence of electronic systems of information has somewhat turned punctuation on its head. We are told not to use commas and full stops on envelopes because these confuse the brain in the Post Office sorting machine. They are counter-productive because they slow down the speed at which letters can be processed. The headings of most word-processed letters come to me without any punctuation. A glimpse through almost any magazine will show that the rules of conventional punctuation are flaunted regularly in the pursuit of a clearer, more appropriate means of conveying information. Is this another example of minimalism in writing? Different-sized spaces, variations in typeface and colour are used to signify the meaning that punctuation once controlled. There is nothing new about this. Modern poets frequently use spatial dynamics to, for example, denote emphasis or symbolise a pause. As fewer words are used so the page is liberated, and the available space redesigned to explore other ways of processing information like, for example visual imagery and the enigmatic uses of 2D space itself. Perhaps a pluralistic society accessing multiple systems of communication demands an easing-off of rigidly held traditional ideas about the mechanics of writing.

Are we to teach children to punctuate and then de-punctuate, and if so, where is each applicable? Is there a new 'spatial' language in which spacing and font style communicate a kind of hidden punctuation implicit in the subtle visual arrangement of words? Is education ready to even begin to discuss how children learn the mechanics of writing in a new age of communication?

The book as container

But letters in envelopes are only one way to conceive these books. There are others . . .

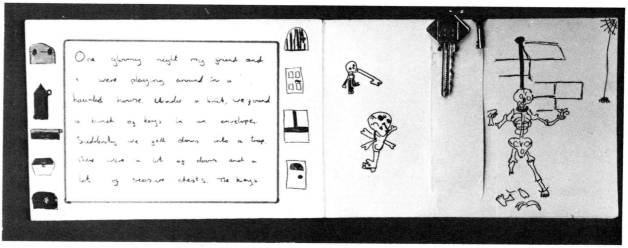

'The skeleton key' (23 × 16) by Christine (10)

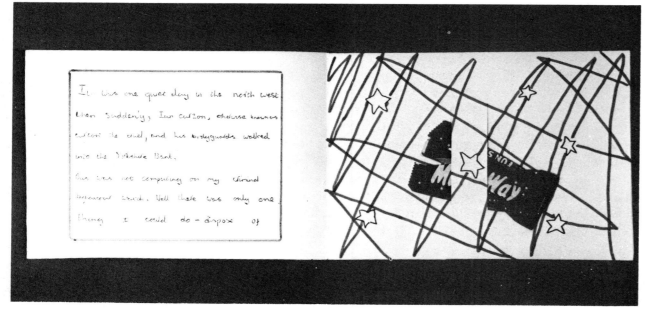

'Milky Way Kid' (23 × 16) by Tony (10)

Both these examples come from the same project and demonstrate that even a throw-away object like a sweet wrapper can be revitalised into the thematic focus of a story. Tony uses a strip cartoon technique for his narrative. In it, Curzon the Cruel, attempting to rob the Yorkshire Bank, is arrested by The Milky Way Kids.

A real bunch of keys makes a bulky package for Christine's book about accessing hidden treasure. 'It never occurred to me', said the teacher, 'that the bunch of keys which had been lying around the house for so long could be used not only as a story stimulus, but find its way physically into the book too!'

The influence of closely observed picture books is evident from the border drawings which illustrate the story whilst leaving the central space for the uninterrupted text. This technique can be found in illustrated books from the medieval period to the present day.

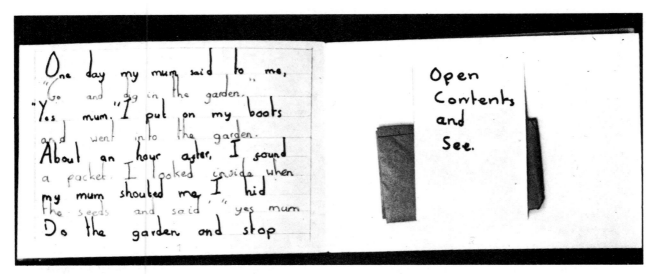

'The seed packet' (15 × 10)
by Carrie (10)

packet of seeds and when her friend joins her she sees there is a message on the side of the packet. It says 'Plant these and see what happens!' They do so, and shortly after a strange plant grows. It is a money plant. The narrative structure to the four pages is as follows:

1 Main character digging in the garden finds a packet.
2 New character examines packet.
3 Seeds are planted and grow.
4 Money appears on the plant.

Carrie said of her writing process:

> 'You couldn't have just ordinary seeds in the packet because that wouldn't make an interesting story. That's why I thought up this idea about a money plant. When I came to the last page I could see there wasn't much space left, so I thought, 'I must write the ending of the story about money growing on the plant and then see what is left over'. So the ending about not wanting my dinner was put in to finish the page.'

This is an even smaller book folded down from a sheet of A4 copier paper (page size A6), yet the contents seem to fit the total area perfectly. Note that at the end of the story there are only two or three centimetres left of the page – a model of planned design or an accident?

How the project was organised

The teacher wrapped a number of flatish objects in envelopes. Each one contained something different. The one illustrated contained seeds; others contained sugar or small beads. Some were sealed so that their contents had to be determined by shaking or feeling; and others could be opened to reveal their secrets. The task given to this year 6 class, which had one envelope per pupil, was to devise a story for a younger audience, using it and its contents as a strategic part of the narrative. The envelope was both a part of the book and the stimulation for it as an object to be explored by the reader. The class brainstormed thematic ideas around which a plot could be woven. The seeds could be used for: curing an illness; replanting the rainforests; or making the most beautiful garden ever seen. They then drafted the narrative in a replica of the finished book (four A6 pages). Attention was given to the presentation, ruled borders and lines for the text as well as ensuring that words fitted the lines without 'breaking'.

Carrie's story is about herself being set the task of digging the garden by her mother. She finds a

The authors involved in this project took their books into the infant part of their school and read them to younger pupils on an individual basis. A teacher described the theatrical atmosphere created by the removal of the seed packet from the book, shaking it, and asking the question, 'And what do you think is in here?' which *was* a performance.

(In a similar project in a Stockport school the books were given to the five-year-olds as a personal present. The younger pupils were then asked to suggest an outline for a story which the older pupils wrote down and illustrated as a story book.)

Variations on a seed packet

I invited a group of teachers on a course to suggest alternatives to seeds as a 'container' stimulus. These are some of the ideas they came up with: coloured threads, pins, paper clips, nut shells, dried orange peel, a Polo mint, a stamp, an earring, a bus ticket, dried flowers, and nails.

Taken a stage further we programmed plots for some of the objects:

Pins These are very special pins because if you use them to hold together material for a dress and then come back exactly ten minutes later, you will find the dress completely sewn together. However, if you go away and forget about the dress, the pins will just stay there and nothing will happen.

Nut shells Squirrels never throw away the shells of nuts when they eat them; instead they carefully glue them together and make them into storage jars. So if you find any nut shells like these, will you please take them to the squirrel bank (you will find the address at the back of this book) so that they can be recycled into storage jars. Thank you.

'It is surprising how stimulating it is to actually have the envelope container in your hand, and to be able to shake, or examine its contents' said one teacher who had developed this idea with her class. 'Somehow, its presence seems to heighten the experience, and give authority to the initiation and development of plot.' To help the visualisation process another teacher designed a number of plot supports which could be planted around the thematic object. For example:

Polo mint

> This is the last Polo mint in the world. Why?
> How did it come to be placed in this envelope?
> Who put it there, and why?
> Was somebody trying to steal it?
> This might look like an ordinary Polo mint, but if you put it very close to your ear and listen you will hear . . .
> Once there was a very old man and all he had in the world was a . . .

If you reflect, even briefly, on the postman book concept, and play with the idea of 'objects which tell stories of fact and fiction' before long you will have arrived at a limitless list of themes across the curriculum subjects.

Take the following items: map, letter, bill, photograph, drawing, ticket, passport, cheque, poster, recipe, menu, newspaper cutting,

postcard, advertisement, and manuscript. At once, from just a few two-dimensional objects there is a built-in environment of narrative story-making and project work possibilities in the humanities and sciences.

After a visit to one of Manchester's museums by a school in Glossop, Derbyshire, the pupils were asked to report on it. Andrew describes the train journey to Manchester, which he illustrates and then uses the tramlines to hold his ticket to the museum.

> 'We met at school then we walked to Glossop station, then we got on the train. We had some food. We stopped at Piccadilly then we got on another train to Deansgate. We got to Deansgate. We walked to the Air and Space Museum . . .'

Another important point to stress is that all of

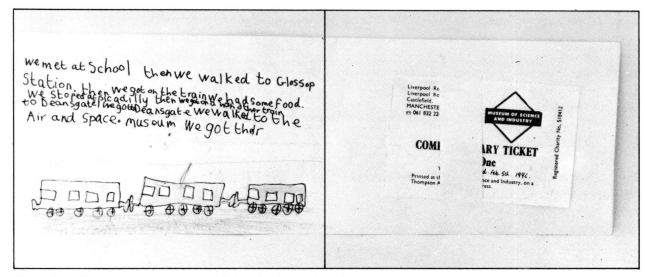

'Our trip to the air and space museum' (21 × 14) by Andrew (7)

these objects can be used in both fact and fiction simultaneously. In *Linnea* (Bjork and Anderson, 1985), the late lily pond paintings of Monet are discussed both as Impressionist works of art and as part of the fictional experience of a young girl. In this beautifully moving book the reader is effortlessly conveyed through two realms of meaning.

A map can be the centre of an adventure story or the central reference of a history/geography/local environment project. Robert Louis Stevenson drew his own map of 'Treasure Island' which he described as the chief stimulus for the plot of his

book. In *A Hundred Acres*, Freddie Mckeown (1991) records in delicately watercolour-painted words and pictures a year in the life of a hundred acres of English countryside. This book, dedicated to the preservation of our countryside, culminates in a large, fold-open map reproducing the ground covered by the book.

In a different vein, a £5 note can figure in a story, or a project on finance or economics (see also *The Mystery Wallet* on pages 42–3 and 98). What better draughtsmanship skills could be developed than simulating the design complexities of paper money? There can hardly be a skill requiring more

drawing acumen than this. The only danger might be if pupils became so expert at doing so they could be arrested as forgers! In *Folded Words and Images* (page 10), I used parts of this project to illustrate what children can learn about complex coding systems through design oriented tasks. The whole book was prepared as illustrated below.

For each pair of pupils engaged on the project two basic 'tramline' books were made except that the last page of the first book, and the first page of the second book had tramlines cut into it as well. The two halves were joined, thus making a book with eight pages and a front and back cover.

Double tramline book

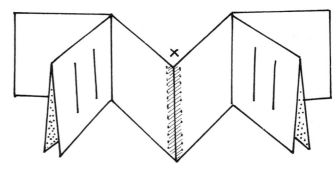

The two halves are joined together by a strip glued to the rear of 'X'.

How the project was organised

The class was arranged into sub-groups with only one table of six children engaged on the banking project. The six were grouped in pairs. 'Real' transactional material was used throughout – a £5

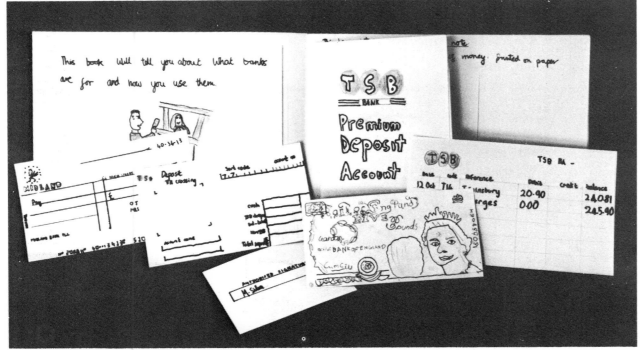

'Banking' (23 × 16) by Emma and Mariana (8/9)

note, blank cheque, bank card, paying-in slip, statement, and deposit account book. Paper had been cut to the same size as the forms and the deposit book was already made up using the 'Hidden Staple' technique (see page 115). The six pupils took it in turn to use the 'real' visual aids. Firstly they lightly sketched out the main structure of the note/form/book, checking proportions by holding the visual aid alongside, above and below their simulated design. Quite a lot of rubbing out and starting again ensued, but a sense of achievement was proclaimed when one or other of the pupils felt they had 'cracked it'. Completed designs were slotted into place, and appropriate captions discussed, drafted and written at the top of each page.

Preparing the whole class
To involve the whole class with this project the teacher had prepared a simple description on A4 paper called 'What banks are for' which supported his introduction to banking, which had been done in conjunction with a 'Question and Answer' sheet. This had headings like 'What do you call the paper slip you use when you put money into the bank?'. Over a period, all pupils completed the project.

Structure
Cover (page 1) – Brainstormed title for book, authors and thematic graphics.
Page 2 – General description of book. Emma wrote 'This book will tell you about what banks are for and how you use them.' Drawing of man depositing money.
Page 3 – £5 note. Caption by Mariana: 'This is a picture of a £5 note. It is the lowest sum of money printed on paper.'
Page 4 – Cheque. Caption by Emma: 'If you have a bank account you can use a cheque for taking money out of it.'
Page 5 – Bank card. Caption by Mariana: 'You use a bank card when you are buying something from a shop.'
Pages 6/7/8 – Deposit slip, statement and deposit account book and accompanying captions.
Page 9 – Concluding copy. Mariana wrote: 'Why don't you start saving and then one day you will be able to use cheques, have a bank card and a bank book.'
Back cover – Copy: 'Read this book and you'll find out about a bank before you even imagined! It's never been such fun!'

In another journey across the curriculum one could arrive in home economics. A project here might comprise recipes for special occasions in tramline 1 and a party menu in tramline 2. Progressively, children could undertake a hotel promotional presentation, complete with logo incorporated into a folded napkin, hotel notepaper, and even a brochure advertising a sauna and swimming pool which could be a more advanced project for a table-group, each with delegated responsibilities and an editor-in-chief. On page 98 in the colour section this idea is shown as the production of one child. Note how the size and character of the objects have influenced the placing and number of tramlines to the page. Rebecca made a list of things to be designed in her imaginary hotel. She was given help in planning these, categorically, into the book form. Sketches preceded the finished designs. The final task was the drafting and writing of the promotional copy. This project took three mornings to complete.

'Birthday menu' (10 × 15) by Rachel (5)
(Part of a 'list making' project by an infant)

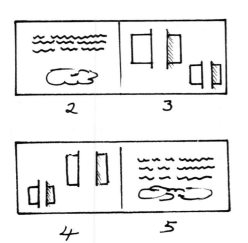

Engineered arrangements of Rebecca's book (see page 98).

*See '**The Hidden Treasure Hotel**' by Rebecca in the colour section on page 98.*

Sequence of planning
1 Promotional features of hotel.
2 Headed notepaper.
3 Business card.
4 Serviette.
5 Sauna club membership card.
6 Facilities and tariff.

Page design
Page 2 – 'The hidden treasure hotel provides you with spacious rooms and breakfast in bed. We also have a swimming pool and sauna club. For an extra £20 we provide a colour TV and computer. All rooms have balconies but it's an extra 50p for a view.'
Page 3 – Letter paper and business card.
Page 4 – Serviette and sauna club card.

Page 5 – 'If you want to hold a business conference, we have a perfect room for it and you only have to pay £5.00. We also have a café which is perfect for business lunches.'
Back cover copy – 'Find out why you should choose the hidden treasure hotel for your stay.'

Asked what she would like her next promotional project to be, Rebecca said, 'A sweet shop.'

The magic of envelopes
Envelopes are wonderfully evocative forms, giving almost as much pleasure as objects as the information they hold. In *A Book of One's Own* I showed a basic (one star) origami envelope. Here is a slightly harder one to make. The end result rewards the effort.

Origami envelope

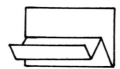

① *Fold portrait in half on horizontal.*

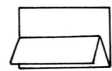

② *Fold top sheet in half.*

③ *Fold top quarter sheet in half.*

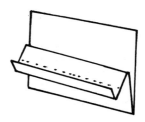

④ *Drop front quarter down and fold up bottom edge to quarter sheet making ⅛ fold.*

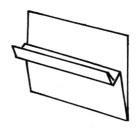

⑤ *Fold ⅛ up again.*

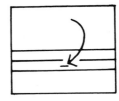

⑥ *Crease down top edge to point shown.*

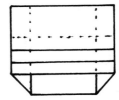

⑦ *Fold bottom corners on diagonal. Crease vertically at points where diagonal reaches base.*

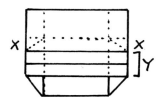

⑧ *Crease angles in panels 'X'. Fold 'Y' folds upwards.*

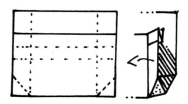

⑨ *Open bottom corners and fold side flaps to centre.*

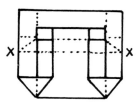

⑩ *Fold down central section at 'X'.*

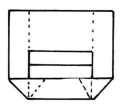

⑪ *Fold outer flaps to centre and drop down bottom corners.*

⑫ *Tuck bottom corners inwards.*

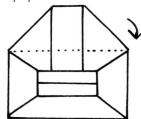

⑬ *Crease diagonals at 'X'. Fold flaps 'Y' down and tuck into envelope pocket.*

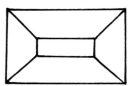

⑭ *Tuck lid inside envelope.*

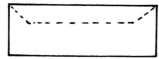

⑮ *Completed envelope.*

Most of the following envelopes shown can be made on either landscape or portrait orientation. Measurements are for A4 size paper.

There are numerous other envelope forms which can be made from a single sheet of paper. Here are five basic ones:

1 Basic tuck-in envelope

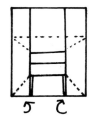

① *Crease 3 cm from top edge of landscape.*

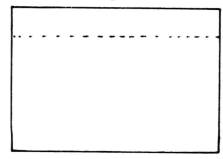

② *Fold 3 cm flaps on left and right sides. Fold diagonals on top corners.*

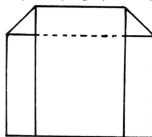

③ *Fold bottom edge to top 3 cm crease.*

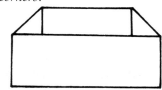

④ *Fold top lid into side flaps inside envelope.*

2 Folded-in envelope

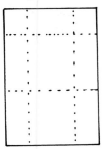

① *On portrait crease left and right sides to centre and 3 cm from top. Crease up bottom edge to 3 cm crease.*

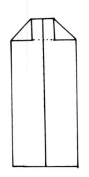

② *Fold left and right edges to centre. Fold diagonals on top corners.*

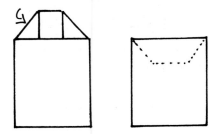

③ *Fold up bottom edge to 3 cm crease. Tuck lid into envelope.*

④ *Completed envelope.*

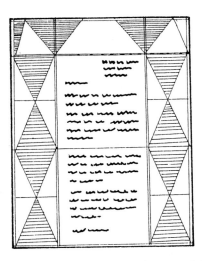

Design arrangement for using envelope as a letter-envelope.

3 Pocket envelope

This is a spacious envelope ideal for holding several objects or bulky material.

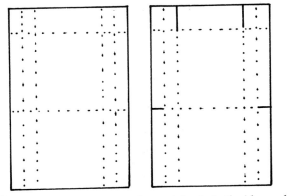

① *On portrait crease two 2 cm strips to both sides and 4 cm to top.*

② *Crease bottom edge to 4 cm crease. Cut as shown.*

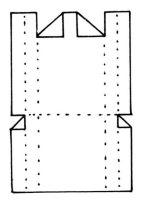

③ *Fold diagonals as shown.*

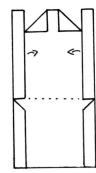

④ *Fold first left and right creases, then fold again.*

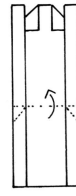

⑤ *Fold bottom edge to top crease.*

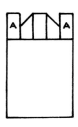

⑥ Tuck tabs 'A' into folded edges inside top of envelope.

⑦ Tuck lid inside envelope.

⑧ Completed envelope.

4 Triangular envelope

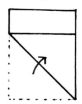

① Crease bottom diagonals on portrait.

② Crease top of square.

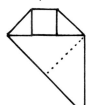

③ Fold in diagonals on top corners.

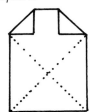

④ Fold up bottom left diagonal.

⑤ Fold up bottom right diagonal.

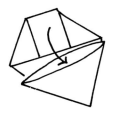

⑥ Tuck lid into envelope pocket.

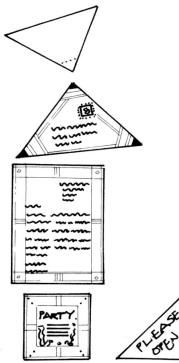

⑦ Completed envelope.

A letter/invitation can be written on the portrait A4 before folding. Alternatively, a smaller square sheet of paper, folded on the diagonal, makes a triangular invitation card.

5 Irregular envelope

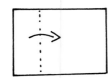

① *Fold short edge of landscape to form square.*

② *Turn square to diamond orientation.*

③ *Fold bottom half upwards.*

④ *Fold bottom left corner to centre of right diagonal fold. Repeat from right.*

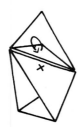

⑤ *Tuck front top triangle behind front flap 'X'.*

⑥ *Tuck back triangle as envelope lid into envelope.*
⑦ *Completed envelope.*

'Swimming party invitation' (8 × 7) by William (7)

'Two stamps celebrating imaginary monsters' (6 × 5) designed by Emily (9)

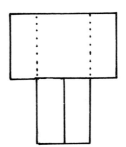

(Celebration stamps enlarged to postcards are available from the larger post offices, and make excellent visual aids for stamp designing projects.)

All the above envelopes could be written in before assembly and so become letter-envelopes, but here is a purpose-built one:

6 Letter envelope

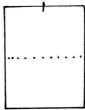

① *Crease portrait A4 on horizontal.*

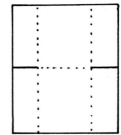

② *Mark top centre and crease left and right edges to centre. Cut as shown.*

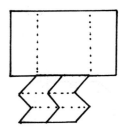

③ *Fold bottom left and right panels to centre.*
④ *Fold bottom section into thirds.*

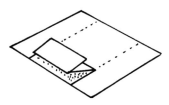

⑤ *Fold bottom section into top section.*

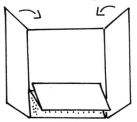

⑥ *Fold top outer panels to centre.*

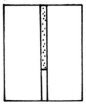

⑦ *Fold up envelope to just above folded letter inside.*

⑧ *Fold in top corner diagonals.*

⑨ *Tuck lid inside envelope.*

⑩ *Completed envelope.*

Invitation cards

'Locked' invitation cards were popular in the Victorian period and have an instant appeal because the unfastening process holds one in suspense. Here are some which are easy to make and, like the envelopes above, they can be used in any of the developmental 'Postman' project work.

Locked cards (slotted)
1 Single lock

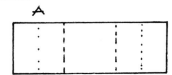

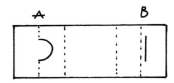

① *Cut landscape A4 in half on horizontal. Crease into three equal vertical panels. Crease right side panel in half again. Draw line 'A' half-way across left panel.*
② *Cut semi-circle in centre of 'A' and matching slot to right side of fold 'B'.*

③ *Fold outer two panels to centre, and inner crease 'B' outwards. Crease top and bottom of 'A' outwards.*

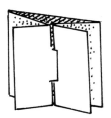

④ *Lock projection on 'A' through slot 'B'.*

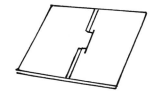

⑤ *Completed card.*

2 Double lock

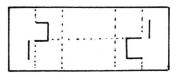

① *Fold as before but cut locks on both sides. Cut slots as shown. The horizontal dotted line indicates that the bottom edge of the left lock should align with the top edge of the right lock.*

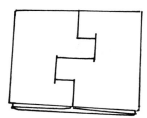

② *Completed card.*

Locked cards (non-slotted)

Unlike the cards above which are joined by feeding a tab through a slot, these cards are joined by interlocking tabs.

1

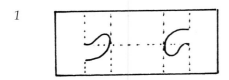

2

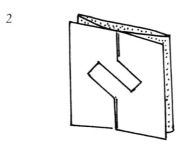

3

① *Curved lock (see 1, 2, 3 above)*

Follow creasing and drawing instructions as before. To ensure that the tabs interlock, line up as shown by horizontal dotted lines.

1

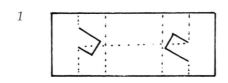

2

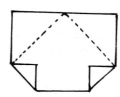

② *Diagonal lock (see 1 and 2 above)*

This is a variation of the lock above. Experiment with other shapes which will lock effectively.

Triangular invitation envelope and card

This activity produces a combination of the origami envelope and an accompanying card. The invitation envelope came about just by improvising with a sheet of A4 copier paper. Do the same and see what you come up with!

① *On landscape, crease top diagonals to centre and fold bottom diagonals from the crease inwards.*

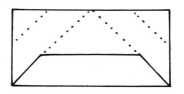

② *Fold up bottom section and fold top diagonals to centre. Fold top diagonals outwards to envelope edge.*

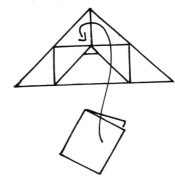

③ *Place invitation card inside triangular pocket.*

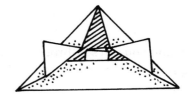

④ *Completed card inside envelope.*

38

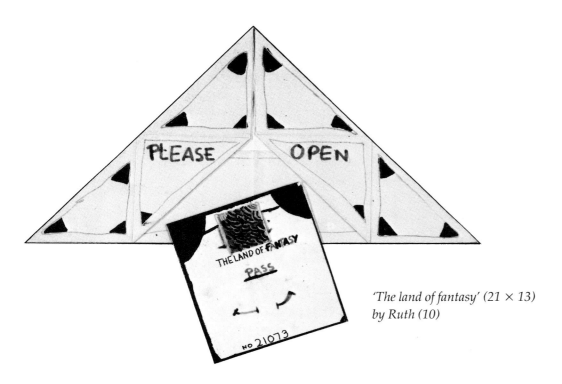

PLEASE OPEN

THE LAND OF FANTASY

PASS

NO 21073

'The land of fantasy' (21 × 13)
by Ruth (10)

Ruth's official pass into 'The land of fantasy' has a surreal quality about it. She described to me how it gave the holder access to an adventure environment similar to Disneyland except that it is all under the ground. She said, 'When the pass is placed inside the triangular envelope it turns transparent and lights up. If you hold it up to the light it glows and you can see through it.' Would a less exciting stimulus have produced such an evocative concept?

By exercising the imagination one might come up with a project which integrates all of those topics already discussed!

Construction techniques
Before moving on, one important factor of these projects must be recognised. With so many books, the way one reads them bears little relationship to the way they are made. One unconsciously turns the pages both as writer and reader. However, the thematic foundation of *The Jolly Postman* – inspired books is inextricably connected to the removable objects through which the story emerges. Pupils start their books by deciding the identity of the object held on the second page, and then journey backwards to the beginning of the book to conceive the story. However many objects are planted in the book in this way, they always shape

the prefacing narrative plot. So the author may well preface the drafting process with the making of the artefacts, replicas and ephemera around which the plot hinges. In turn, these forms can influence the way the story develops. When the book form conditions the writing which goes inside it in the classroom, many of the accepted norms of the process writing model may need rewriting!

Before leaving the rich environment of 'postman' books, here is another, very different structure which uses the tramline idea.

Book with diamond cover

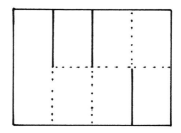

① *On landscape, crease half and half again on the vertical. Crease panels 2–4 on the horizontal. (Do not fold panel 1.) Cut panels as shown.*

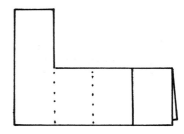

② *Drop top panels 2–4 behind bottom panels.*

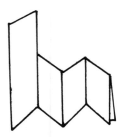

③ Concertina pages. Turn book to front cover.

④ Crease top panel diagonally to right.

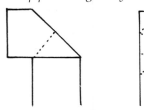

⑤ Repeat creasing to left.

⑥ Crease top corners into centre on diagonal. Crease centre of large diagonal on horizontal.

⑦ Fold diagonal section inwards and bring down top corners so that they tuck under the diamond that is formed on the title page.

⑧ Apply glue to reverse side of diamond and fasten into place on cover.

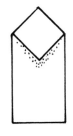

⑨ Completed book.

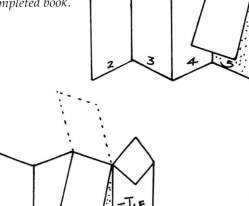

Page organisation showing lifting flaps on pages 5 and 8.

'London' (front) (9 × 19)
by Alex (8/9)

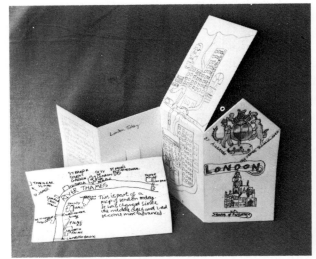

'London' (back)

This book, as engineered, presents a cover, plus seven pages. At first glance it looks like a basic four-fold concertina, but the inclusion of lifting flaps and pointed cover makes it into a form with inventive possibilities (because of the complexity of the cover engineering, this book form was made for the pupil). The book falls into two conceptual halves corresponding to its two sides. The brief was for pupils to select a theme which had a before/after, then/now duality symbolised by the two sides of the form. Alex selected London as his theme, and arranged the pages as follows:

Page 2 – Opening description of book – 'This book is all about one of the great cities of the world – London.'
Page 3 – Brief outline of the size of London and the financial circumstances of its inhabitants.
Page 4 – (folded, in tramlines) Drawing of London's buildings in Edward VI's reign.
Page 5 – Drawing of medieval London on extended flap showing progress of the Thames from Westminster Abbey to the English Channel.
Page 6 – (reverse of book) 'Turn over this page to reveal a map and a drawing of London today.'
Page 7 – (folded, in tramlines) Map of London today showing railway stations. The caption tells us that it has become '. . . more advanced.'
Page 8 – On the lifted flap the same line drawing of the Thames as before is shown, except now surrounded by high rise buildings.

The final task involved designing the cover. Alex used several history books from the school library to help him with his project. The diamond head to the cover seemed the perfect place to draw the royal crest. He spent a long time on this, carefully planning the detail. The rest of the cover is designed with confidence – well arranged drawing and lettering and an unusual way of recording his name around the bottom two sides of the engineered diamond. Alex's book, like so many others shown here, needs several pages of analysis to do it justice. As we look at it we sense that it is a 'successfully completed' task, but like Sarah's autobiography discussed in detail at the beginning of this book, what that means is the skill to organise a complex interrelationship of writing, drawing and design tasks. Finding the right words to describe in one sentence not only what the book is about, but to make it compelling, is a professional skill. Compare Alex's drafts for page 2:

'If you go to London, then you will see what is in this book.' (Not well phrased.)
'If you want to find out about London a long time ago and how it is now, then you can have a look in this book.' (Still not well phrased and too long.)
'This book is all about London and how it used to be and how it is now.' (Much better, but second half too long.)
'This book is all about London.' (Now too brief.)
'This book is all about one of the great cities of the world, and that is London.' (Much better, but poor ending.)
'This book is all about one of the great cities of the world – London.' (Good!)

Alex has made several books before, so he is used to thinking in a 'book' way, placing separate ideas on each page in a sequence to make a unified whole and 'listening to what the blank book-form is trying to tell him'. Although he is probably not aware of it, his mind is sorting out for him what is best said with words, and what with diagrams (the map), and drawings (medieval buildings). Alex is a pupil who can be 'left to get on with it', needing help only with the cultivation of his text. He is a slow worker, but also a surrogate teacher, for the pupils sitting around him learn, not only from watching him draw, but from the *manner* in which he works.

From the illustrations in books he has used to research London, he has extracted the essence of, for example, the decorative façades of houses in the middle ages. He has learnt from developmental drawing what to put in and what to leave out. Here the techniques of writing and drawing are astonishingly similar, for both are a refining process of cutting away what is unnecessary and revealing the bare truth of the matter. But aesthetics is interwoven into this process, for without the imaginative modelling of words, or the sensitive shaping of line drawing, all that is accomplished is a bald statement, and although it may communicate in some factual way, it does not 'hold' the reader or viewer, so it is then lost, even forgotten, before it has been assimilated. In communication terms it has failed. Aesthetics *is* the psychology of communication. And Alex is gradually becoming a master at it.

By redirecting the 'Postman' approach down another channel other possibilities present themselves . . .

Six-year-old Richard was very impressed with his origami wallet and spent most of the morning giving out imaginary money to other children. One child, clearly wanting to emulate this philanthropy, opened her pencil case and started to distribute imaginary money with the same generosity. 'That's not a wallet,' said Richard indignantly. 'Look, you can't get your pencil case in your pocket, so it's not a wallet!' (He demonstrated the truth of his claim).

Wallet book 1

① *Crease 8 rectangles. Cut first three panels on landscape horizontal. Remove bottom left panel and trim the next panel as shown. Cut slots as shown.*

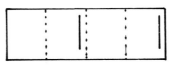

② *Drop top four panels over bottom four. Concertina top panels to right.*

③ *Fold left 'lid' over pages and lock through slot on back.*

A sideway move from the letter/parcel/package concept is that of the wallet/bag/attaché case. These books differ from the postman examples in that the replication is of a different type to that of an envelope or simple container. A wallet book can simulate a real wallet with fold-over clasp and pockets for cash and credit cards. The structure of the folds alternate pages of text/illustration and engineered openings. There are four possible pages for text and artwork, although the slotted pages could be used for this purpose as well.

*See '**The Mystery Wallet**' by Amanda in the colour section on page 98.*

Amanda's story, written in the first person, begins by describing how she finds what at first she believes to be a brown piece of cardboard; but which, on closer inspection, turns out to be a wallet. Inside is a £10 note and a credit card. A bully tries to take it from her but she runs home and shows it to her mother. At once they take it down to the police station. Returning the next day they find that the wallet has been claimed and that the owner has left £50,000 for Amanda! This 'honesty is the best policy' morality story is told as the reader's scansion progresses, not only through the text, but through the removable contents as well.

How the project was organised

The class folded down, cut (with scissors) and refolded the basic book form from A3 paper. The process was guided by a combination of chalkboard diagrams and live-action demonstration. The only parts of the book which required a cutter (the slots) were cut by the teacher after school. A visual aid showed which pages had to be prepared for text. Templates 1 cm smaller than the page area were provided for each table group, and these were drawn around following the visual directions:

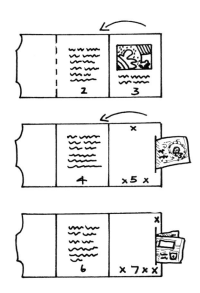

Book planning strategy. To prevent objects falling from the wallet lightly glue points marked 'X'.

By referring to their books, it became clear that they had four pages for text. But what story would be told there? Amanda's book shows how selecting the wallet's contents leads the imagination into designing a plot. A hospital appointment card and raffle ticket will produce a very different story from a pop concert ticket and a blood donor card. Moreover, the kinds of documents people carry with them make statements about their values. A person who habitually carries a kidney donor card in his/her wallet indicates a consideration for others which could become the central theme of the wallet book.

Transforming the wallet

The wallet form when opened out in another pattern offers many variations:

Wallet book 2

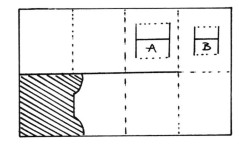

① *Crease and engineer as for Wallet book 1, diagram 1, but without slots. Engineer doors as shown. Door 'A' should be larger than door 'B'.*

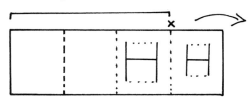

② *Fold top panels over bottom ones. At point 'X' swing first three top panels over to the right.*

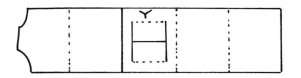

③ *Opening door panels in centre will reveal the smaller door beneath it. Lightly glue down the edges of the superimposed panel 'Y'.*

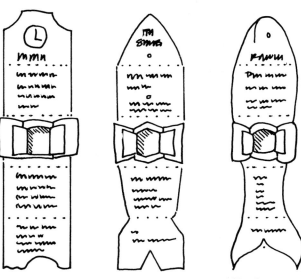

Turned to the vertical orientation a range of book themes can be created.

See '**A Grandfather Clock**' by Sarah Jane in the colour section on page 99.

These 'wallet variations' were all engineered by the teacher, but the folding down was done by the pupils. The double doors in the middle of the clock add that little bit extra to this book form – something the standard hanging concertina book lacks. Children notice the doors immediately on first viewing. Of course they can open them first, but they know that that is cheating, and besides, what is inside may not make sense without previous textual information. So there is no alternative but to read the story down the folds, the anticipation growing as they near the doors! By writing for a younger audience, Sarah Jane is being taught to build this psychology of the architectural book-form into her planning. Moreover, the book demands that she has two pages of text leading up to the door, and one after it. The pages are prescribed rectangles of a few centimetres. Minimalism once again rules.

On page 1 (written in the first person) the author sets the palace scene with a grandfather clock and a cuckoo appearing from it. On page 2 she is frightened by it, which makes the Queen laugh. Page 3 is the engineered double doors with a cuckoo on a paper spring fastened to the bottom sheet. Page 4 explains how the Queen shows Sarah Jane around the palace, but as it is the clock which intrigues her the Queen decides to take it apart so she can see how it works.

Preparation
A template, 1 cm smaller than the page, was drawn around three times in Sarah's drafting book so that her draft was constructed in the same area as the finished book. The edited draft was written inside the template area on the finished book, firstly in pencil, then after final proofreading, written over in ink. This completed, the artwork to the clockface and the opening doors were created along with whatever other decorative motifs were felt necessary.

See **'26'** by Lawrence in the colour section on page 99.

The central section of Lawrence's rocket book shows the control room of his craft and the inner and outer doors.

See **'Wristwatch'** by Rosie in the colour section on page 99.

Rosie's wristwatch is different from most of the work by other pupils engaged in this project because it is conceived horizontally. This, of course, is because of the nature of the theme itself. The idea of a watch came from the thematic brainstorming which involved the whole class at the beginning of the project and from which the clock and rocket ideas came.

Rosie has given herself two panels for text, one for artwork, and the remaining three for watch face and the joining buckle of the strap. In her story, 'Miss Fiddle' fiddles so much with her watch that she breaks it. As it is no more use as a watch, she decides to live inside it. The reader tunnels through the inside workings of the watch (the

'Holidays of a life time' (15 × 11) by Shelley (9)

engineered central section) and in the bottom part Rosie has drawn Miss Fiddle's living quarters. A giant, discovering the watch, takes it to be repaired and poor Miss Fiddle is so shaken by the journey she has to be taken to hospital. (The full-page illustration is of her lying in bed in hospital.) When she returns home to the watch she decides to do her own DIY and work on the interior design of her home.

'Enjoy Yourself at Wales. Why not enjoy yourself at jolly old Wales. This holiday will suit you if you like living in a cottage, horse riding, walking or fishing . . .'

This book is simply two strips of paper folded into a concertina with the ends joined. Shelley has designed the book folds into an original holiday advertising brochure – Disney World USA, Tenerife, Blackpool and Wales.

Concertina greetings card

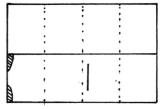

① *Crease eight rectangles and cut in half on landscape horizontal. Trim envelope lid on first bottom rectangle and cut slot on third panel as shown.*

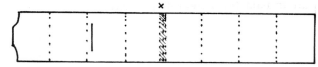

② *Join both parts together with a strip glued to the back of 'X'. Fold down and tuck lid into slot.*

Collecting seaside greetings cards which are sent to you, or which pupils bring from home, provides a resource bank of project starting points. Nothing is more effective than the real thing!

Origami wallet book
It was seen earlier that there is an inexhaustible number of origami envelope designs. The same could be said for origami wallets, purses and boxes. Here, one wallet form is discussed as part of an unusual book creating project.

In the wallet shown opposite, the surface area has been textured with a pattern before folding. This shows how the technological process can extend to fabric-design type work.

Origami wallet

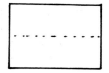

1. *Crease on landscape horizontal.*

2. *Fold top and bottom edges to centre.*

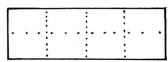

3. *Turn over and crease vertically in half. Crease sides in half again.*

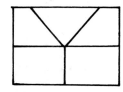

4. *Fold corners on diagonal to horizontal crease.*

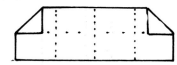

5. *Fold left and right panels to centre.*

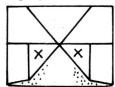

6. *Raise flaps 'X' each side of bottom centre on the diagonal.*

7. *Fold inwards on horizontal and tuck flaps 'X' over corresponding diagonal folds.*

8. *Fold vertically in half to complete wallet.*

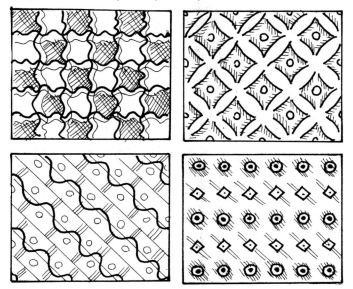

Explore making decorative patterns on paper before folding.

45

How the project was organised

This project was organised collaboratively. Five tables of six pupils produced one wallet book each.

Process

1 Introducing the wallet – Through chalkboard diagrams and repeated, stage-by-stage demonstrations, the teacher helped each table to construct an origami wallet. As with so many paper technology construction processes described here, trials were made on junk mail, graduating to large sheets of newspaper, and finally to A2 cartridge paper. (Even a large sheet of paper produces a relatively small wallet). One leader was appointed to each table, but everyone in the team was expected to have some part in either the trials, or the final product. (The last stage of making the wallet is the hardest, and the teacher played an interventionist role here.)

2 Romancing the wallet – The class now discussed the wallet concept. What are wallets for? Why do people carry them? What kind of things do they carry? Already familiar with *The Jolly Postman*, it did not take the class long to connect the wallet theme to a plot. Could a story be told through the articles in the wallet? What kinds of things could we learn about the owner by examining its contents? A list was made of possible items. These started conventionally: a letter, photograph, money – and a fairly ordinary person began to emerge – but then ideas like maps, secret messages and envelopes with foreign addresses began to be suggested as the class raised the plot to a higher level of invention. Ideas fell into two main categories: a person on a secret mission, or an explorer making a big discovery.

The teacher said that the story would not be told through a written narrative, but *implied* through the objects. The reader would be invited to make connections between them – like a detective searching for clues in a classic whodunnit – and therefore make up his or her own story. A brainstorming session provided a stimulus to the table groups designing their plots, from which objects emerged: garment label, receipt, letters with parts torn out, telegram, crumpled piece of paper bearing a cryptic note, a key, an address, a handkerchief with embroidered initials, and a bill for purchases.

See '**The Lost Wallet**' in the colour section on page 99.

The development of the project is now told through the work of one table.

3 Delegating tasks – Beth was a natural leader and suggested, as a main object in the wallet, a letter which would contain an important piece of information about a discovery, but crucial information like the address and location would be missing.

> 'Dear . . ., Found skeleton in North America . . . morning.
> Come . . . quickly . . . and . . . meet me . . . on . . . From . . .

This task didn't take long, and so Beth was able to also make another item – an aniseed ball sweet wrapper.

Martha responded to this idea by designing a telegram in code. (You can break the code by moving each letter or numeral one letter backwards.) The first few words 'Efbs K. Ibwf gpvoe voefshspvoe djuz . . .' becomes 'Dear J. Have found underground city' when translated.

The owner of the wallet is now clearly 'J', and so Rose took this up by addressing a postcard to 'J' referring to a secret document. On the reverse is a picture of a fortress-looking building on an island which clearly has some meaning to the developing plot. As Rose works quickly, she had time to make another object, and this was a drawing of a prehistoric creature. This also is addressed to 'J', but the implied discovery of a rare species is made more exciting by its name being burnt out! (This was done by the teacher using a match.)

Jane's contribution was the design of a 'Free' coupon for 'Mittie's mouse food', and Jennifer completed the constructing task by designing labels off (*a*) a garment (deep sea diving wonder suit) and (*b*) an ice-cream maker machine.

All the ideas were drafted first (words and sketches), and edited by other members in the group. Changes took place here. For example, someone said that Jennifer's ice-cream maker didn't look like one, which led to its re-design. The title design fell to the person who finished first.

4 Constructing plots – The originality of this type of 'book' is that everyone who investigates its contents *makes* the story because it is not written down. As the wallet book was completed, the groups had to analyse the person contained within it, and what story or stories were revealed.

The wallet could contain several different plots, or the same story told in different ways, depending on the order in which the items were placed. A bus ticket could be the most important item, or of no significance. In nearly every case, the most significant factor (e.g. identity of the wallet owner) was never stated. Wallets were passed from table to table for new interpretations to be made by children wholly unfamiliar with the wallet contents.

As a celebration, each table had to 'perform' their wallet to the rest of the class in an interactive way, inviting interpretations from the audience as they removed items. The groups were encouraged to present their wallet books as if they were reporting the results of detective work. One group did this with a class in the next age group down, and made the whole thing into a piece of theatre. The following is a brief extract of one version of the wallet 'story' under discussion, recorded at a classroom performance:

> 'One day we [the table group] found this wallet. We tried to find out who it belonged to, but inside it we found a letter with the person's name torn out of it. This is it. [Letter held up.] This letter came from someone who knew *that* person, and had found a skeleton, and was trying to contact the owner of the wallet . . . We also discovered that the wallet's owner likes aniseed balls (sweet paper held up to class) and deep sea diving (label shown). We think he needed the diving suit to search for hidden treasure . . .'

At the end of a similar project, and after a performance, Janet said, 'I don't ever want to write an ordinary kind of story again'.

Are these ideas just novelties, an amusing way of designing a writing and designing scheme?

A teacher, referring to these book forms, said to me recently 'They take the sting out of learning to write'. But is that all? Aren't they all as relevant to a knowledge of linguistic and visual language as scientific investigations are to scientific knowledge?

Today through the post came a wallet containing travel documents for my trip to Amsterdam. There were in all fourteen separate printed objects in this wallet. It is as much a book as a DIY manual is a book. The only difference is that this survival package is best supplied in separated units, each designed to service the need it provides. The methods of arranging words, symbols and illustrations on different shapes and folding patterns of paper have been arrived at by a design team asking the question: 'What is the most effective way of communicating this information in a wallet of such-and-such dimensions?' A book of stapled pages would be ineffective here. The complexities of modern living, of air tickets, customs regulations, insurance and a host of other things to make a holiday run smoothly necessitates a newly invented 'book' of unattached parts unified by a wallet as the 'book cover'.

Pop-up wallet
Pop-up paper engineering is one of the most engaging ways of introducing technology to children. In this project with four- and five-year-old children, Beryl, their class teacher, combined this with a science project investigating plant growth.

Pop-up wallet

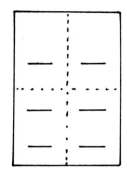

① **Base** *Crease portrait on vertical and horizontal. Cut slots as shown. Fold top panels behind bottom ones.*

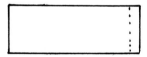

② **Pop-up form** *Cut a strip of paper, the length of which is slightly less than the height of the base panels above. Crease one edge.*

③ *Fold over other edge and glue on folded crease.*

④ *Cut away strip through bottom of both pieces of paper leaving central tabs.*

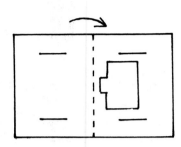

⑤ *Lay pop-up form in centre of right base panel and glue bottom tab to it approximately 2 cm from centre. Apply glue to top tab, and lower left base panel onto it.*

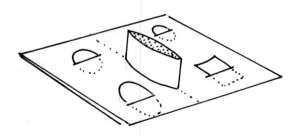

⑥ *Allow glue to dry, then raise pop-up into 3D position.*

The four slots provide pockets for holding objects related to the project discussed here (seed, rain, soil, sun). Likewise, the front and back cover slots can be used for securing and projecting forms.

Front cover (seed packet)

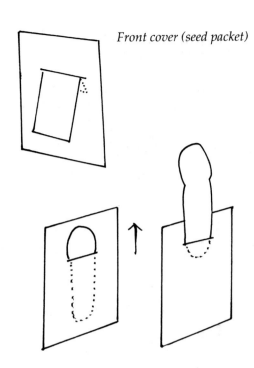

Back cover (growing plant)

Covered over pop-up

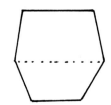

Flap

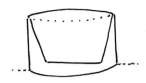

Flap attached to pop-up.

By attaching a flap to the back of the pop-up form, a lid can be made to cover it. This also prevents the wallet's contents from falling out when closed down.

See '**My Book of Flowers**' by Rebecca in the colour section on page 100.

How the project was organised

Over a period of a week or two, basic pop-up wallet forms were made for each pupil in this reception class. The assembly process was shown to them, and individuals drew artwork on the flat forms, and helped Beryl in some of the simpler engineering operations, like pressing the folded base down after gluing, pausing, and lifting the form into three dimensions. Concurrently, the class explored the conditions of growth, the progress from seed to plant, and made a practical record of their observations from plants seeded and growing in the classroom. Garden tools were on display too, together with charts and illustrations of growth forms.

Beryl ingeniously adapted the wallet form into a plant pot shape to accommodate the theme. It was organised as follows:

Front page: slot to hold seed packet.
Inside left: slot to hold soil and below that slot for sun form.
Inside right: slot for rain, and below that slot for seed form.

The pupils drew the seed, soil, rain, and sun and these shapes were cut out for them. A slot at the top of the back cover enables a fully grown flower to be raised above the confines of the page. Through only a limited time working with pupils, Beryl used the pop-up reality as a concrete way for pupils to experience the growth process:

Teacher: What do we put in the pot first?
Pupil: Soil (pupil places cut-out in the pot).
Teacher: Then what needs to go into the pot?
Pupil: Rain and sun (rain cut-out placed in pot, followed by the sun).
Teacher: And what is the last thing we put in?
Pupil: The seed (pupil places seed in pot).
Teacher: Now let's turn to the back cover and watch the plant grow. (Pupils take it in turn to raise the plant pull-out above cover to simulate growth.)

Beryl was convinced that by simulating the whole pattern of growth in this way, pupils would be more likely to understand the process than by using a more formal, descriptive method. Also, of course, these pupils had their introduction to pop-up engineering this way, and basic design and labelling experience too.

Six-year-old pupils working on their books

'I want to make a fold-down model of the universe to put inside my book' said an eight-year-old to his teacher. 'Will you show me how to do it?'

Books with integral pockets

Pocket book

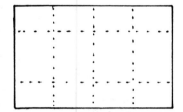

① *Crease landscape vertically in half, and half again. Crease top and bottom edges to centre.*

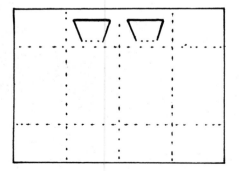

② *Cut flaps as shown.*

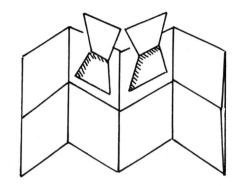

③ *Fold top and bottom creases to centre. Concertina pages and raise flaps.*

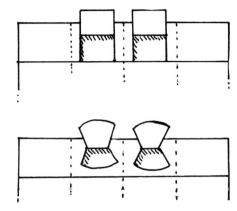

Alternative designs.

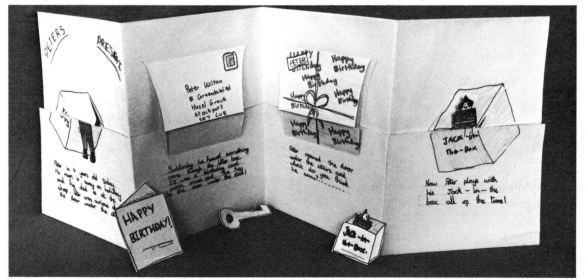

'Peter's present' (16 × 23) by Emma (10)

In this book form pockets are made by the horizontal folds of the central two pages. Pockets are also provided on the outer two panels but as these open along the outer vertical edges they are unsuitable as containers.

Emma had already worked on a book of this style in its most basic form and so for this, her second pocket book, she was encouraged to be more adventurous. The idea of letters which had been the thematic basis for her first book reappeared in her planning but, together with other children working on the same project, she brainstormed a plot structure.

Teacher: Envelopes are containers for letters but what other containers are there?
Pupils: Boxes, tins . . .
Teacher: Think about things which can be opened on a hinge.
Pupils: Doors, cupboards . . .
Teacher: Make a list of all the places you can think of which are hinged in your home . . .

From the long list of cupboards in the kitchen and bathroom, and boxes under the bed, the class had to select four, corresponding to the four folds of the book. Emma's list was Jack-in-the-box, birthday present, letter, and a door under the stairs. The teacher played a game in which an improvised story connected the four items in one order and then in another. Very different plots can be constructed in this way. Eventually Emma settled for the following permutation: door under the stairs, letter, a birthday present (unopened), and birthday present (opened).

This produced a story in draft form about Peter who is curious about the door under the stairs. His Mother, who is away from home, sends him a birthday card and inside the envelope is the key to the cupboard. Inside he finds a parcel which, when unwrapped, is a jack-in-the-box.

The book was designed for a much younger audience and so the text and the information contained in the pockets were kept to a minimum. The teacher cut the pocket openings to Emma's specification and the jack-in-the-box was glued into the final panel to prevent it being lost.

In a group of infants who were shown a book similar to this, and allowed to handle the contents of the pockets, including a paper key, one child said, 'This key opens a magic box that I've got', and then proceeded to open an imaginary box and tell her own story about it.

This book is a celebration of boxes, many of which are engineered as envelopes. Inside each envelope is a flat paper form which one can construct into a 3D object by following the instructions on the box lid. These include a dice to play a game with, a basket for chocolates, and paper sculptures.

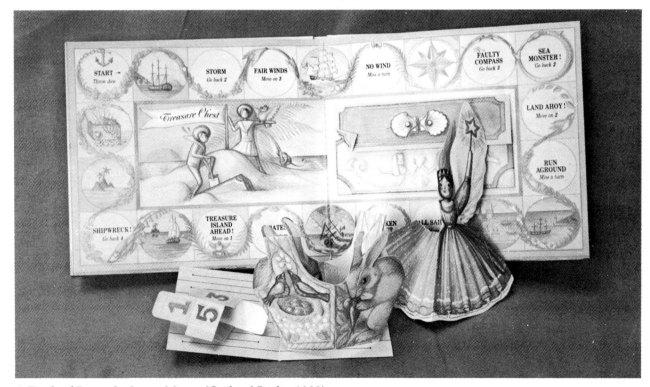

A Book of Boxes *by Laura Mason (Orchard Books, 1989)*

'Christina's piano exam' (16 × 23) by Catherine (10)

Catherine's story, told inside a single folded form, was inspired by *Dinner With Fox* (Wyllie and Paul, 1990). The fox, attempting to entice a hare and a pig to his house, leaves an invitation in their respective mail boxes. The mail boxes open so that the letters can be removed and read by the reader. An important experience in Catherine's life at that time was being successful in a piano examination. She describes the sensation of entering the examination room – 'Christina felt her tummy turn upside down as she opened the door. The room was empty except for a large piano and a set of tables with the judges there . . .' She thinks she has failed the examination because she made a mistake, but has she? A letter arrives. She invites the reader to open the postbox and see for him/herself what the letter contains. Inside there is a tiny certificate which says 'This is to certify that Christina Royal has passed grade 1 on the piano'.

The real and the imagined

Like the invitation card of Lucy's book (page 25), and Amanda's credit card (page 98), Catherine's music certificate is another example of non-chronological writing within a design context. Take design away, and the writing task loses its clarity.

These book forms process the child's organisational thinking so that the gap between fictional prose and real-life situations is narrowed. It is the successful combination of the 'real' in imaginary situations which is the foundation of good story writing. The imaginary and sometimes bizarre world of the story writer is conditioned by the everyday paraphernalia of our social ambience – newspapers, dentist's appointment cards, maps – which, however fantastic their context, must adhere to a logical and recognisable structure to be accepted by the reader. The more authentic in content and design a menu or 'money-off' coupon looks in a story book, the more it will be 'believed' in a make-believe way. And the nearer the pupil will be to acquiring confidence in using these same concepts reoriented into, for example, running a business or setting up a home later in life.

In the world outside school, alternating styles of verbal communication are common. Even in the intimate task of writing a letter to a friend one may start with a description of a person one has just met and finish with directions of how to get somewhere: '. . .then take the A32 to the B1121. Carry on for two miles then . . .' Finding words to define a complex journey by road brings into focus not only a combination of words and visual symbols but the most economic means of arranging both on paper.

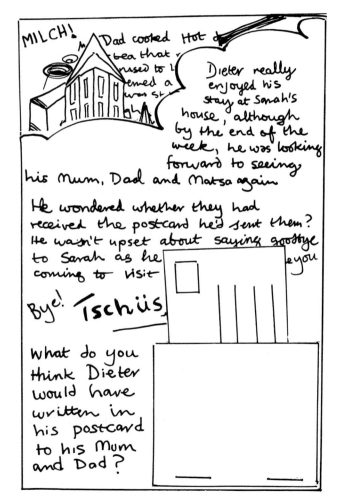

Page from 'Dieter's Trip' (14 × 20) by Helen Philips

Sensitivity to the technologically conceived page, the design concept woven into that form, and the verbal and visual content which makes the invisible form visible, is essential to the author's mastery of communication. Without the eye of the designer, words are just dead objects on the page.

This illustration, part of a book made by a PGCE student, has been designed as a stimulus for both learning German and making a book. The pocket on the page holds a removable postcard and an invitation to write on it.

See ' George and the Letterbox' by Sally Kemp in the colour section on page 100.

This is part of another book made by a (non-art qualified) PCGE student as a stimulus for a class of children to make books. It is important that these books by students should be shown here. They are, of course, a creative and engaging way of stimulating a class, but they do more than that; they embrace children in a shared experience. The student-teacher is saying, in effect, 'I really loved making this book for you, and I want you to experience what a thrill it is to make a book, especially when you have someone in mind you are making it for.' And however good commercially published books are as a guide or stimulus to children, they are never as special as the book 'I have made for you'.

I am fortunate enough to own Sally's book and I have used it several times, and in different contexts, when working with children. The following project illustrates its influence on a group of middle juniors.

Origami pocket book

Make two basic origami books (see page 114).
Lightly draw in door on page 3, and large openings on pages 5 and 7. Open to full sheet and engineer openings.
Fold down books again.

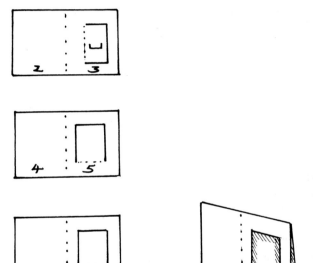

To make pockets:
Drop down panels on inside, fold at bottom edges of page, and glue to page behind opening.
Lightly glue outer edges of pages to prevent work falling out.

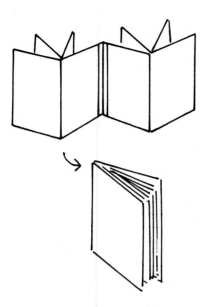

Glue both books together with a strip applied to the rear of the join.

This form is based on the basic origami book (see page 114). By cutting openings on three sides and folding down, under and up the inside of the page fold, a pocket is constructed without any other additions being required. By joining two such engineered books together, four pockets and two pages with engineered doors are possible.

The theme is a week in the life of Lucinda Letterbox, told through the letter-box deliveries made to her each day. The book form provides six pages, one for each working day, Monday to Saturday. The pages for Monday and Thursday are designed as doors with engineered letter-boxes, like Sally's book, and the remaining four days as pockets. One of these joined origami-style books was made for each table of six children in the class.

*See '**Lucinda Letterbox**' in the colour section on page 100.*

Several days prior to this project the book was described to the class. They already had experienced *The Jolly Postman* and so were primed to the mailed letter concept, and the variety of data letters can contain. It was explained to them that their postman-type book would go one stage further and include everything that can be delivered through a letter box. The class now had to decide who should be the character in the house. Could a name be made from the theme? Eventually the class came up with:

Lucinda Letterbox
20 Lime Tree Grove
Littleton
Redbridge
RE7 4BQ

A few minutes' brainstorming produced a long list of things that could be delivered through her letterbox each day. Daniel added a bomb to the list, which didn't surprise me for, try as hard as I may, I can't wean him off stories in which all the characters shoot or knife each other. The brief was then for the pupils to bring into school, over the following days, items such as junk mail, envelopes, postcards and magazines in preparation for the project.

How the project was organised

The collection of objects brought in included predictable things like pizza advertisements and local newspapers. Several envelopes came in, including lots of brown ones and – at the other extreme – cobalt blue envelopes on bonded paper. We discussed how different types of mail came in these envelopes and that you could tell the classification of contents by the colour. I had with me a collection of gas bills and the like, and so there was a brief discussion about bills in general and what sort of costs there are in running a house and how you pay for services. As a 'warmer' I read them part of the memorable poem *Night Mail* by W. H. Auden.

The tables were now organised into groups of six pupils, corresponding to six days, so that each pupil knew which day was his/hers. Monday and Thursday pupils worked directly into the two halves of the book, for at this stage they had not been joined. These were the door pages, and from the photograph one can see the influence of Sally's book on them. As this class had made books before, and developed illustrations, the challenge of designing the interior of the house, and exterior view through the front door, was well received as the artwork shows. Anna has made sure that her picture-making is a rich experience for the eye – a flowered carpet design, table with lamp and letter, and patterned door. As might be expected, Sally's minuscule newspaper in the letterbox was the main attraction of the page and much time was spent on its preparation, design and folding. The text accompanying Monday's door says 'This book is all about Lucinda Letterbox and the things she gets delivered to her each day'. The text for Thursday says, 'On Thursday Lucinda had delivered to her a magazine.' The four other days consisted of whatever 'delivered' objects the individuals wanted to include in their 'day'. This was discussed to avoid too much repetition. A range of origami envelopes (see page 32) of different sizes and types had been prepared. As a purist I like everything to be home-made, but there is no reason why ordinary envelopes (perhaps re-used ones with stickover labels) shouldn't be used in projects like this, especially if this is your first voyage into book art.

I was particularly pleased with Mark's pizza advertisement. He is dyslexic but has not just copied the advertisement but added some ideas of his own. This notion of 'adding something' was a condition; every pupil had to change the format they had in front of them in some way. This could be *à la The Jolly Postman* – perhaps a play on words – or changing the wording of the sales copy. One letter on police headed notepaper informs Miss Letterbox that the TSB Bank is pressing charges of theft against her. The letter finishes 'You can expect to hear from the court soon. Yours sincerely P.C. Coup.' Others in a more serious vein, and in brown envelopes, inform Miss Letterbox that her electricity or telephone calls have come to so much and should be paid at once. There are postcards from friends on holiday all around the world, including Barcelona and Cyprus, all extolling the virtues of sea and sand and suggesting that Lucinda comes out and joins them. Developing lettering skills was particularly

noticeable in tasks like simulating taxi advertising cards and illustration design in magazines. Mohammed made a good realisation of the front and back of a newspaper and accurately recorded the interacting blocks of copy and artwork or photographs. Here are some of the comments made by the children during this project:

> 'She's not going to like getting this bill.'
> 'I think I'll send her a letter from her best friend in Australia.'
> 'I don't think the postman will be able to deliver a parcel this size.'
> 'Can I send her a letter about how to recycle junk mail?'
> 'I'm not going to tell anybody what's inside this letter.'

The biggest problem with projects involving as many as six pupils to one end product, multiplied by five tables, is the sheer exhaustion of answering ten queries at once. For however many visual aids you produce, and however many reinforcements you make about the most basic of tasks, a quarter of the class never seems to know what they should be doing. At the end of the weekly project sessions I had to collapse in the staff room over a cup of tea! But the rewards are great. You can imagine my pleasure as the book began to take shape and finished artwork (for everything was a 'design' of some sorts) was 'delivered' through Lucinda's letterbox.

Another fact of collaborative work, in addition to all the social and idea-sharing advantages, is that whatever you are doing gets done so much faster than independent work. Consequently one is never confronted with a decline in interest which bedevils so many complex projects like this one.

This project belongs to that family of writing and design which is multi-layered. Not only will it make these children pause and reflect for a second or two longer than normal on the mass of paper thundering through the door each day and its purpose, and indeed the wastefulness of most of it, but the nature of the communication *language* itself. Projects like this are at their best when they relate progressively to other tasks, perhaps developmental letter writing or designing a class or school newspaper. The vastness of the subject matter means that there can hardly be a curriculum area which isn't affected, either in content or method of working, by one or more of the tasks essential to 'Lucinda Letterbox'. In this context, the class had recently made a visit to the early industrial community at Styal, a National Trust property in Cheshire. One of the tasks they had been given was that of imagining themselves to be an apprentice writing home describing his life in the mill. Another contemporary project involved them in designing an anti-litter poster. Both these examples of curriculum content show how different aspects of a particular task can be interrelated across several themes.

For a moment I thought four-year-old Ella was going to try to eat *Sam's Sandwich*. She brought it up to her face, opened her mouth wide and then, looking at me, an enormous grin came over her face as she laid the book down.

Bearing in mind children's preoccupation with food, the concept of a book in food form must be a winning theme. The sandwich is 'made' for the book because its layering is so easily simulated by the folds of the concertina form in the horizontal position.

Sandwich book 1

① *Crease to eight rectangles and cut three panels on landscape horizontal.*

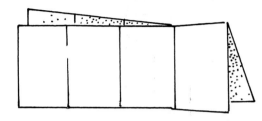

② *Fold on horizontal.*

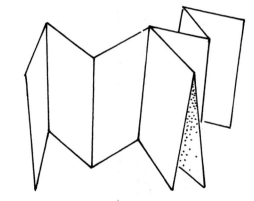

③ *Concertina pages each side of central fold.*

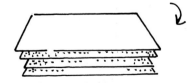

④ *Lay book on landscape position. This provides a book with eight working 'sandwich' pages.*

The project discussed here was carried out with a reception class. Four basic sandwich book forms were made from an A2 format, one for each of the groups. A range of salad items was prepared – lettuce leaves, radishes, spring onions, hard-boiled egg, tomatoes, cress – one for each in the group, along with A4 sheets of paper and crayons.

See *'Sam's Sandwich'* in the colour section on page 101.

The first part of the activity was to examine David Pelham's *Sam's Sandwich*. The unfolding of the contents and the discussion of what they were (including the red dollop of ketchup) preoccupied the children for an inordinate period of time. Each one of the group wanted to close down and re-open the lettuce and cucumber *et al*, a lengthy process, and so it began to seem that they would never get round to making a response to it. Through this tactile experience the book was transformed from two to three dimensions and back again. Eventually they were distracted by the real vegetables and encouraged to draw them. The teacher explored the characteristics of each species with them:

'Jade noticed at once the seeds in the middle of the cucumber, but Tom needed help in seeing that the long slender spring onions started dark green, but became lighter towards the end of the stalk. Ella went straight into drawing the cheese almost without assistance, but Alex found the cress a real problem to draw – a task I sympathised with, as cress, unlike the other shapes, isn't really a shape at all but a conglomeration of small grass-like forms . . .'

So this observational drawing task of integrating shapes with colours had been stimulated by the objective of making a *Sam's Sandwich*-type book. When complete, the teacher cut around the forms, and with the assistance of each child, glued them into the book. Ella finished before the others and so was appointed to design the cover. By looking closely at her piece of wholemeal bread (already beginning to turn up at the corners in the heat of a July classroom) she observed 'It's got holes'. And this knowledge of bread, not as a solid flat object but something resembling a sponge, is reflected in the way she has drawn the form.

Ben drew the cover of the book on a separate piece of paper which was glued into place. An interesting post-activity event was the teacher showing these books, one page at a time, to the class 'on the mat'. As the pages were turned, individuals were asked to describe the food drawn there – 'And what did Sam put in the sandwich next . . .?'

Sandwich book 2

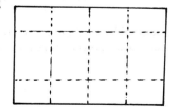

① *Crease four equal vertical panels on the landscape. Crease top and bottom edges to centre.*

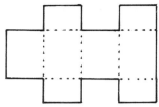

② *Cut away panels 1 and 3 from top and bottom sections.*

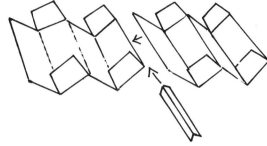

③ *Fold top and bottom panels to centre and concertina pages vertically. Make as many sections as required and join with glued strips to underside.*

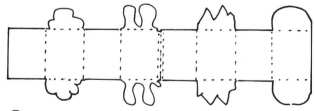

④ *Vary page contours to match themes.*

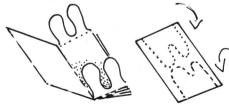

⑤ *Concertina the completed book down, folding raised forms inwards.*

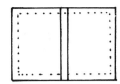

⑥ *Measuring card cover.*
Height – height of book pages plus 1 cm.
Width – width of closed book pages plus 2 cm. Add 2 cm for spine. (More width if book runs to several sections.) Glue back edges of front and back pages to inside cover.

⑦ *Completed book.*

The structure of this sandwich book is more complex than the previous project because it is designed for children capable of a more advanced way of thinking and designing.

See **Jill's Sandwich** by Rebecca in the colour section on page 101.

Rebecca planned out her narrative one page at a time so the book could have stretched to almost any size. Like the reception class, Rebecca's class were shown *Sam's Sandwich* and then invited to prepare a similar introduction and to prepare the artwork for the first page. As this extends beyond the parameters of the closed book, quite a large drawing of edible objects could be placed here.

Therefore the teacher suggested that the artwork should be bold and representative of the food itself, for example sausages look shiny and textured. From the perfectly acceptable initial food-stuff, it was suggested that, like *Sam's Sandwich*, the sandwich's contents should become progressively macabre. The class, of course, warmed to this suggestion without exception! In Rebecca's sandwich book, Jill, the sandwich-maker, adds all manner of unpleasant ingredients to her mother's sandwich, like books and big dollops of mustard. The final ingredient, multi-coloured toothpaste, shows how much thought she has given to the appearance of toothpaste (e.g. the marbled surface). Finally, Jill's mother, having tasted the sandwich, runs out of the house and down the street. The synopsis on the back cover reads 'This is a book about a nasty girl called Jill who made a terrible sandwich for her Mother.' Like Ella, in the reception class book, Rebecca illustrates the texture of bread on her book, but this has come from an analysis of David Pelham's artwork and not real bread itself.

How the project was organised

First of all sections of the sandwich book were made available to individual members of the class, and the different structures of the book were discussed, including the engineering structure and the narrative structure.

Process

The children began to draft the narrative. Once completed, they transferred the draft to the first section of the book and began sketching the art-work (real objects could be used here, or even illustrations from magazine sources). They then completed the artwork using colour and pen line drawing. The next stage involved drafting the second part of the story and then transferring the second draft to the second section. Final illustrations were drawn until the book was completed.

The sections of the book were joined together by a glued strip on the *inside* of the sections (to hide it from view). The cover design (using *Sam's Sandwich* as a guide) and back page copy (synopsis) were on separate pieces of thin card, folded to form the cover. The book sections were then glued to the inside cover. The last stage involved each table group taking their books to Year 2 classes and then 'performing' them.

'Look, I've made a sandwich book.
If you've never seen a sandwich book
you're in for a surprise.
Look what this sandwich has got inside!'

Children need to be taught the skills of 'holding' an audience. Some are born to it of course, but most need to be shown how to project their work. With the class in question, pupils were paired off to perform their work to one another, and some were invited to use the whole class for their rehearsal.

Watching children read their stories to an audience, especially when they have rehearsed it well, is one of the joys of teaching. So many seeds are sown here. For some pupils, this experience will set them firmly on the road to successful professional writing much later in life; for others it is the first step into the realm of learning to communicate orally; and for others, it is the growth of self-confidence which will be the most important aspect. A teacher colleague expresses it well:

'Ordinary day-to-day speech serves its purpose reasonably well. We are generally understood. But telling or reading a story brings into play a kind of communication which is unique for the one being communicated to. Both performer and receiver are lifted into the transformative zones of the imagination, and held there in a dialogue which is magical.'

The above two examples show how 'architectural' books can be made in developing stages of engineering complexity. In the second book some pupils were confident at cutting around the contours of the illustrations, while others needed help from the teacher at this stage.

'Tom's sandwich' (16 × 23) by Pratic (11)

Two years on from Rebecca we see how a budding illustrator uses developed drawing skills (sensitive use of line and shading; good sense of design) in the same task. The opening out of the page enables the artist to be less restricted than the standard small book format.

Other possibilities

There are numerous other book possibilities in the sandwich form:

A plate book A circular shape of paper with fried egg, beans, chips, etc. as hinged pages which can be lifted to reveal what is under them (e.g. 'nasties', secret messages, other kinds of food). Beneath those, another page for the narrative.

A trifle book Concertina pages each dedicated to a different layer (e.g. custard, strawberry jelly, blancmange), and then a story woven through them about a surprise birthday party.

The toothbrush book
To conclude this section I have included a toothbrush book. This idea came to me when sipping coffee over *Ben's sandwich* in a Manchester coffee shop. I used the caffeine to assist me in the brainstorming task of inventing a book like it. What else looks like a book but isn't one? I came up with some pretty crazy ideas, but one which stuck was this idea of a toothbrush. The bristles look something like pages and the handle, well, not unlike an extra long binding. The idea was reinforced a few weeks later when I discovered a shop in Amsterdam which sold nothing but toothbrushes. I also remembered that in my

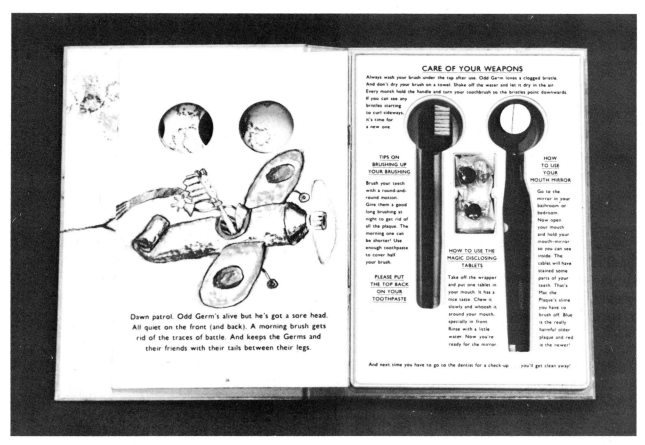

Cleanaway! *by N. Salaman*
(Pan Books, 1984)

collection of unusual books I had somewhere a book with a real toothbrush inside it . . .

It was *Cleanaway!*, a story book which warned of tooth decay through nasty characters like Sticky Sam Sweet and Mac the Plaque. The good guy is the toothbrush in a panel at the back.

So came into being my own version of a book built around a toothbrush. The best way to display them is probably to lean them against a vertical surface, or even to pin them to it. The only disadvantage with the latter idea is that you can't then hold the book, and part of its message is in holding it like a toothbrush as you read the story in the 'bristles'.

Toothbrush book

To make book:

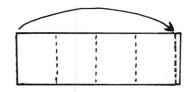

① *On end of horizontal strip crease 1 cm. Fold left edge to crease and fold again.*

② *This makes four pages plus a strip for gluing book sections together.*

③ *Make card cover following instructions as for Sandwich book 2.*

④ *Cut card strip slightly narrower than spine width and 8 cm larger than spine height.*

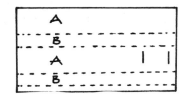

⑤ *To make toothbrush handle. Make card handle approximately book height × 4. Score card so that A = A, and B = B. Add 1 cm or so as a gluing strip. Cut two slots as shown. The distance between them should be 1 cm more than book height.*

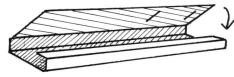

⑥ *Fold scored edges and glue lid to strip.*

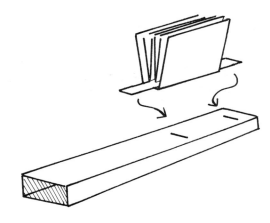

⑦ *Slot card strip through book spine. Join to handle by slotting strips through handle slots. This enables the book to be detached and read minus the handle.*

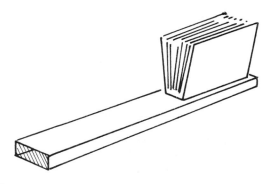

⑧ *Completed book.*

See both **Clean Your Teeth** by William, and **Priscilla at the Dentist** by Meinou in the colour section on page 102.

William's story is in three parts of narrative with matching illustrations. An outline of the narrative is as follows:

'Jon never cleans his teeth. As a result bugs live in them and their chewing gum eventually sticks Jon's mouth together. The fire brigade has to be called out to unstick his teeth.'

Meinou's story begins:

'One day Priscilla woke up in a miserable mood. Her mouth felt horrible and dirty as it usually did. She knew perfectly well why this disgusting taste always got into her mouth in the night. She NEVER cleaned her teeth . . .'

Meinou continues by describing how Great Decay Slimers built tunnels in Priscilla's teeth. One day her parents took her to the new dentist who gave her a ride in his chair and then said, 'Open sesame'. Inside her mouth he found all the creepy

'Toothbrush books' by William and Meinou

crawlies, but she liked the dentist so much that she promised him she would take good care of her teeth in future. On the back cover Meinou has written:

> 'This fabulous book has given pleasure to children all around the world and has been translated into 36 languages. The object of the book is to influence children to brush their teeth regularly.'

Both William and Meinou have used the toothbrush handle as an area for design. William has drawn a large elongated mouth with the title in the middle, whereas Meinou has treated all four sides of it in cartoon fashion. Both these ideas were suggested to them.

How the project was organised

The concertina book itself is easy to make. A worksheet can show the constructing stages. To make the construction easier, cut the paper to the correct width but leave the concertina folding to the pupil.

Process
The story was drafted to fit three templated pages. The edited version was written into the book one page at a time with matching illustrations drawn in. Next came the cover design and back page synopsis, lightly drawn on to the cover. The cover design was completed and the pages glued into the cover. After this the artwork needed to be designed on the handle in a flat state. The handle was glued into three dimensions, and the book spine glued to the handle. (In these last few stage pupils will need assistance in making a good finish to the 'book'. Gluing the handle together neatly needs patience. It would be a pity to spoil hours of writing and illustrating the story only to have it attached to a handle which was unevenly made and oozing with glue.)

Clearly, a project like this fits well with a health programme and is a very effective visual aid for story 'performance', designed for an audience of children of almost any age. In a discussion, Susan (aged eleven) was asked if she thought that the toothbrush book would make younger children want to write. She replied: 'I think that they would want to make one like it, and then when they had an empty one given to them it wouldn't look finished if it was empty, so they would have to write something inside it.' She was then asked if she thought it would stop them wanting to write in more 'ordinary' books: 'No, because they know that it's not a real book. Just something very special like a birthday present.'

'One day I'm going to live in a house like this.'
(An inner-city Manchester child
referring to her house and garden book.)

The recurrent theme of the book as an aesthetically and spiritually conceived building is explored here not so much as a metaphoric image, but as a model of the basic principles of domestic architecture. Later (page 93) I show a project in which ten-year-olds explore their homes room by room, using a visualising technique. Here, however, the starting-point has been to dress the empty shells of houses, and sometimes gardens, with that which has not been seen, but imagined, and thus created on (or rather *in*) paper, for the essence of these book forms is three-dimensional. Of course, such an activity is more than the sum of its parts as any interior designer soon finds out. It is not simply where to put what and matching shapes and colours, but what looks best, where and how one object relates to another. It is in the composition of pictures that one most notices the barrenness of some children's image making. The drawing of a room interior which has precious little other than the solitary picture on the wall and a vase of mis-shaped and indefinable flowers on a table must grace the walls of most primary schools at some time or other. The tragedy is that children go on drawing for the rest of their schooling like this, and if they ever attempt drawing after, for the rest

of their lives too. Yet how does one open the eyes of children to the potential delights of their home surroundings?

Here are a range of approaches to the theme explored by children from widely different cultural backgrounds and domestic environments. In every case it is the simultaneous discipline and freedom, implicit in paper forming, that has structured the framework underpinning the work.

Over several years I have produced over twenty ways of folding paper to resemble a house or house and environment in some form or other. Each one suggests what is to go inside it, not only because the shape and construction of rooms vary, and so need different design strategies, but because the layering of pages replicates the layering of interior space.

House card 1

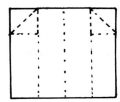

① *Fold portrait in half horizontally. Crease vertically in centre and crease left and right to centre. Crease diagonals on top corners.*

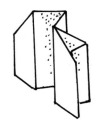

② *Internalise side folds as on page 85. Fold to concertina.*

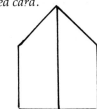

③ *Completed card.*

Closed position (house front)

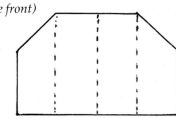

Open position (house interior)

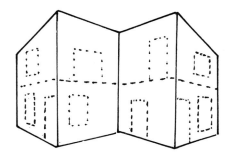

Layout suggestion as a guide for pupils planning proportions of doors, windows and furnishings.

Illustrations as secondary sources of imagery

There is no substitute for direct experience of real objects, but there are circumstances when secondary images like photographs and graphics can show children the richness of our architectural and design heritage. Alun's school is in the heart of Manchester's southern Victorian suburbs and several pages from *Interiors* magazine illustrating that period were shown to the school's top infants. Briefly the teacher talked through the detail of what they were looking at – doors and windows with rounded architraves and central keystones, rooms with moulded cornices – and then the 'exterior' drawing task started with the cards closed down to the shut position. The teacher drew a faint horizontal line through the centre (both inside and out) as a guide distinguishing 'upstairs' from 'downstairs'. This is a valuable pathfinder for emergent graphic artists who lack the spatial awareness to pre-plan page areas. The class was divided into five tables which the teacher visited in rotation. It was therefore some time

later before the next input was possible. For those who had drawn the basic form of their houses, the card was opened up and the interior design began. Pupils could line up the outside door and windows with the inside walls. More time was needed to discuss the interiors, but the theme was brainstormed – chairs, tables, clock, table-lamp, fireplace, radio, pets – and the pupils left with the brief of designing a lounge and a bedroom.

(What was particularly interesting with this experiment was that approximately thirty per cent of the class drew the schematic 'windows at four corners' and therefore nothing of the design input had been internalised by them; whereas the remaining pupils were cognizant of the design input in varying degrees with Alun coming in the top ten per cent of 'design awareness'.)

'My birthday house' (11 × 16) by Alun (6)

House card 2

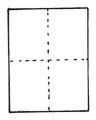

1. *Crease portrait into four panels.*

2. *Fold on vertical.*

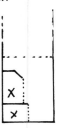

3. *Cut as shown through double thickness on bottom panels. Ensure that cutting does not extend beyond half-way across panel.*

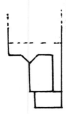

4. *Hinge forms 'X'.*

5. *Press back flat again.*

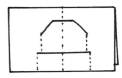

6. *Drop top panels behind bottom ones.*

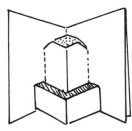

7. *Slowly close card towards you, helping the central 'X' forms to pop up.*

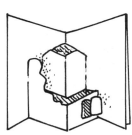

Variation on basic design

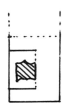

Pop-up design as in Stephanie's book.

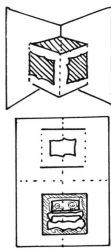

Drawing artwork.
Open pop-up pages and draw pop-up interior on inside of folded page.

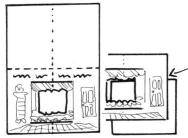

To draw artwork on pop-up page either open up to full sheet, or insert paper sheet in folded card to avoid spoiling artwork beneath.

'This could be yours' (14 × 19) by Stephanie (6)

The basic ninety degree pop-up form from which this design is derived can be made easily, indeed I have seen some six-year-olds cut and fold them themselves. However, the cut-out central panels do need the use of a craft cutter.

It was from one of the *Interiors* magazines referred to above that the idea for this house card came. A four poster bed shown as a double spread linked in well with a current 'Houses in the past' project with this class, but was given an advertising slant as the caption indicates. The group discussed how you would make a bed sound attractive and then listed possible one-liners all starting with 'Wouldn't you like . . . a very old bed? . . . a bed like a house? . . . a very posh bed?'

Stephanie's 'Wouldn't you like to sleep in a bed like this?' took some beating. Notice how observant Stephanie has been in drawing opulent bedroom furniture, wallpaper designs and the drapes of heavy fabrics from magazine sources. This is in no way 'copying', for her choice from a range of several illustrations and advertisements has made this a creative design of her own.

House card 3

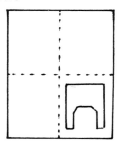

① Crease portrait to four rectangles. Cut house form on bottom right panel.

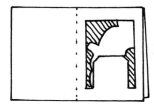

② Drop top panel behind bottom one. Draw tree forms through panel and cut away sky area.

③ Fold on vertical. The cut away sky space now provides the stimulus for artwork on the inside right panel. This strategy creates a near, middle and background.

Birthday card (13 × 19) by Phoebe (6/7)

This is one of several card and book forms reproduced in adjacent pages which are dedicated to Alun, whose birthday (as we have seen) occurred during the period in which these projects were implemented in a Manchester classroom. They symbolise the close, personal identity which should be at the social centre of a school class, and which is the driving force behind so much individual and interactive learning.

The effect of the 'layering' of spatially designed pages already referred to is seen in Phoebe's book by the imagery assigned to each of the three layers – foreground–house; middleground – trees; background – sky. Although the 'depths of field' in this greetings card are in relief form, they nevertheless symbolise the territory of *real* space. When the card is opened, the sky area seen through the front cut-away hovers above a different composition: flying kite, bird in tree, magic carpet. This task has stretched the imagination of a child, just approaching seven, in a highly concentrated period of no more than half a morning.

House card 4

① *Crease portrait on vertical and fold on horizontal.*

② *Cut house form through both left side panels.*

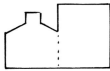

③ *Fold on vertical to make two spatial layers.*

④ *By opening house form fold, four pages are available for text/artwork.*

'I love my family' card (10 × 14) by Hana (6)

This card is a reduced version of the one above and therefore less conceptually demanding. The outer frame and middleground layering have been omitted so that only the house and garden are projected. Hana discovered that, because of the way the card is folded down, the house form is contoured on four pages. She asked if she could dedicate each of these pages to the four members of her family – Fatima, Mona, Mum and Dad.

House card 5

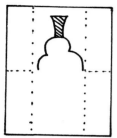

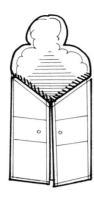

① *On portrait, crease left and right edges to centre. Crease horizontal on side panels only. To make tree, cut inverted tree form in top middle panel. Remove hatched section.*

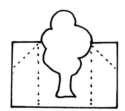

② *Drop top half of page over bottom half. Crease diagonals to top corners.*

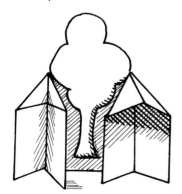

③ *Internalise the side panels so that the triangular forms are folded inwards.*

Closed card   *Open card*

Preliminary drawing for Ben's birthday card

Birthday card (11 × 24) by Ben (6)

This last card can be seen in variation form on page 88. The structures of both books are the same: what differs is the internal cut-away forms. The tree shape which is created here suggests a park to Ben, hence swings and bicycles, but in the ecological terrain of the book form on page 88, the tree has been used to convey a very different meaning. The park theme was finally developed in the gate on the outer panel which was suggested to Ben by his teacher. He was given some help in planning the vertical and horizontal lines, but he did all the finished linework himself.

It is interesting to compare Ben's preliminary

design work with the finished card. In the former the imagery is unadventurous. How did this change come about? The teacher discussed with Ben the activities which could be seen in a park by asking him what he would like to play on in that situation. The rest of the table joined in by making suggestions. Through just a brief verbal exchange, his visual memory produced the rich composition of the final card.

Inwards and outwards

Ben's book shows how some folded paper forms trigger narrative journeys which start on the inside and conceptually work outwards, and others, like Mark's cupboard book (page 73), begin on the outside and develop inwards.

House book 1

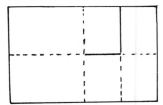 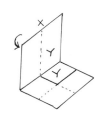

① *Crease landscape to four rectangles, and crease right edge to centre. Cut as shown.*

② *Raise left of centre panels vertically.*

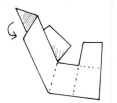 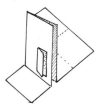

③ *Fold 'Y' round on hinge 'X' to form front and back of house.*

④ *Completed book.*

House book 1 variation

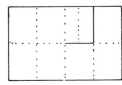

① *Engineer as House book 1, but with the addition of a fold on the top, right of centre, panel.*

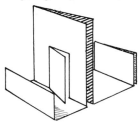

② *Swing round 'X' as before. Fold up back two panels (garden shed), and front one (folded in half) to make garden fence.*

(back view showing garden shed)

Teacher's visual aid (front view)

'Happy family house' (10 × 15) by Jane (6)

The two top A5 folds stand upright to form, on one side, the exterior of the house, and inside, the interior. The remaining A6 panels can be divided between front/back garden artwork and text.

The books which follow are unlike the greeting-card type (on page 68) because they are engineered in a right-angled position and stand on the table top.

How the project was organised

Basic book forms were made for the whole class by a parent giving a much-welcome hand. A mock-up design on A2 format showed the distribution of space to interior rooms (downstairs/upstairs), garden and writing areas. One work table was set aside for 'house books' and the pupils, in groups of six, spent roughly one afternoon each week working on them in rotation. Some children wanted to spend more time on their houses and as several parents operated a rota system as 'helpers' every pupil was able to complete his or her book over about a ten-day period. The stimulation technique, apart from the book itself was (a) for the teacher to make a class scrapbook album of photographs of domestic furnishings and objects culled from magazines, and (*b*) to discuss 'homes' in the daily 'sharing' time during the project period. At strategic points the teacher showed the children patterned cushions, vases, an old clock and the like from her own home. She then discussed with them where in the home you would most expect to find them.

Process

Stage 1 – Using this combination of techniques the class began to classify the basic rooms of a house and how they corresponded to the book form. These were drawn into one room at a time and no pupil could move onto the next room unless the teacher had seen it first. This rule of completing an illustration and discussing it with the teacher before moving on to the next one is one I have seen used effectively with children as young as three years of age. It is so easy to trivialise artwork and miss seeing it as the scientific and aesthetic task it is.

Stage 2 – Now attention was directed to the house exterior. The pupils were reminded that the house had a lower and an upper floor and so the windows and doors on the exterior had to correspond to them. Most were not yet at a stage where they could conceive windows and doors synchronising on both sides of the paper form.

Stage 3 – Then followed the garden artwork to front and back of the house after a discussion on how they might differ from one another. The pupils were encouraged to do this with the house in the vertical position so that they could experience the spatial relationship of house to garden *'in situ.'*

Stage 4 – Finally came the writing of the narrative into the remaining two panels. In fact this was the culmination of an on-going 'Who lives in your imaginary house?' dialogue throughout the project.

What has Jane learnt by making a house book? – The stage-by-stage task has obviously developed a sequencing ability, but what the book form has done uniquely is to enable her to see, in spatial terms, how objects in rooms, and rooms comprising houses, are knitted together to make a whole. Further, the garden areas grow organically from the house and the windows belong to it, architecturally. Compare Jane's house front to the standard windows-at-four-corners schema of most children at this age and you will see what I mean. Notice, too, the variety of curtaining and drape patterns, and you begin to see what a colossal stride forward into realism this piece of work is, enabled by the empirical experience of something akin to an architect's model.

See ***Silly People in Silly House*** by Shelly in the colour section on page 102.

Shelly is Indian and her cultural heritage comes out richly in her house book. I asked her if she had seen any reproductions of Indian miniature paintings of palaces and she said no, but there is something of seventeenth century Mogul art in her bedroom design. Comparing the front exterior of the house with Jane's house front, we see how

much more information has been recorded here. The curtains are hung on brass rings over wooden poles. The door, with elaborate stained glass panels, supports a fan-shaped architrave. A love of detail and exuberant colour is evident everywhere, matched by the description of the occupants, Mr and Mrs Ganore. The character of each room is described and the idiosyncrasies of the couple revealed. The style of presentation is almost journalistic, for example, at the end she writes, 'We thank Mr and Mrs Ganore for their kindness in letting us see their home.'

I asked her why she had written the text as reportage. She said it was because she became so engrossed in the house through the process of making the book (she worked on it every evening at home), that when she came to drafting the story she felt like a visitor 'looking in'. I asked if it was her own home, but she said it wasn't, although she implied that some decorative elements may have been derived from there.

Shelly made the book form herself, with assistance, using a diagram worksheet and a pair of scissors.

Nadia is also Indian although her book is unrelated to the previous book. The paper-engineering technique differs considerably from the previous one because the form is opened out as a series of superimposed rooms. The form was given to her already engineered. Referring to the people in her house book, Nadia said, 'I want my family to be a happy family doing lots of things all over the house. I want all of them to be very busy and very happy.' I sensed that making this book was for her more than the sum of its parts.

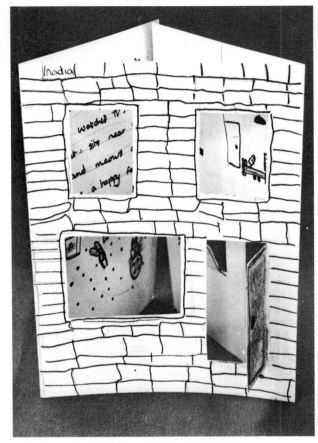

'The happy family' (17 × 23) by Nadia (9)

In all these projects one of the roles of the teacher has been to stretch the imaginations of children by 'making visualised journeys' through everyday situations and environments. Perhaps all of us need to stretch our own imaginations in this way, and to experience the poetry of 'seeing as for the first time' that which is all around us.

Superimposed house book

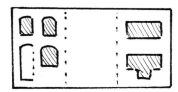

Crease sheet (approximately 30 × 15 cm) into three equal parts. Engineer as shown. The left side panel represents the house front and the right side panel an interior wall. The middle panel becomes the inside back wall.

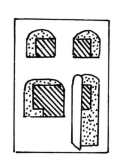

This can be developed into a structure embodying any number of rooms all of which are seen, in part at least, when the structure is raised into the 3D position.

House book 2

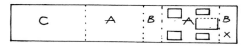

① *Cut strip roughly corresponding to the proportions shown. A = A, B = B, C = A + B. Crease scored lines and engineer openings.*

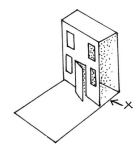

② *Raise into 3D position. Glue 'X' to base.*

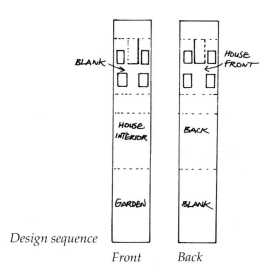

Design sequence

Front   Back

Teacher's visual aid

See **Mystery House** by Patrick in the colour section on page 102.

Patrick's *Mystery House* was inspired by the visual aid shown above. The cut forms were given to all the pupils in his class, but they had to draw in the garden and wall divisions from chalkboard diagrams. Each room in the house had a specific meaning for him in the mystery story he composed, while drawing the artwork. The stage-by-stage planning of room interiors, a cupboard here, a table set for a meal somewhere else, were concrete references underpinning a narrative structure.

Another book form which resembles house books in some ways, but which has been used in other contexts, is the cupboard book . . .

'Will you make me a cupboard book with a secret door leading to a garden in the back, please?' said six-year-old Judy.

I cali the following technique of folded paper 'the cupboard' style because the book pages open outwards from the centre like the doors of a cupboard.

Cupboard book

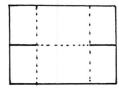

① *Crease landscape on horizontal. Crease left and right edges to centre. Cut central outer panels and fold on horizontal.*

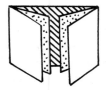

② *Close outer panels inwards.*

③ *Open book.*

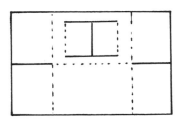

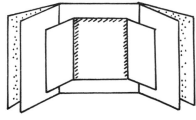

To add an extra set of doors engineer as shown and fold top section in front of bottom one. Open central doors.

As many constructions open in this way it provides an excellent stimulus for a whole range of projects.

Ways of interpreting the cupboard book . . .

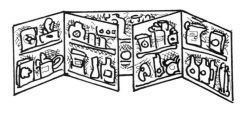

John Goodall has evolved a style of telling visual stories by alternating half pages with whole ones. On the half pages the main imagery which tells the story is drawn, while the whole pages provide the environment. In this way the reader tunnels through the book (half-pages are turned more quickly than whole pages) and experiences an

'Alun's surprise' (18 × 14) by Mark (6)

almost cinematic effect of movement and space. Although the techniques he uses, for example, in *Creepy Castle* (Macmillan, 1975) are different to these 'cupboard' books, nevertheless they both explore similar concepts.

How the book was organised

This book form was made for a whole infant class but its introduction was staggered to smaller group arrangements over two days. The teacher 'performed' the book as follows:

'These are the doors of the cupboard.' (Opens outer doors of book.)
'What's inside the cupboard?' (Sweets, wellies and rainmac, presents, games.)
'And look, (opens inner door) there's another "secret" door in the back of the cupboard. Who or what is in there?' (More presents, a witch, a prince, candy floss, a monster.)

Process

The process involved:

1 Deciding the book (cupboard) theme; designing and captioning the outer door.
2 Thinking about the objects to be drawn on the next four panels; starting at the two central ones and working outwards. Pupils were required to show the teacher the central panel drawings before moving on to the outer ones.
3 Determining caption to inner door and side panels; designing this into the page.
4 Caption and artwork to the inner panel.

From discussing the interior, Mark decided that his was to be a refrigerator. At first he started to draw in food at random but his teacher decided that this was an uneconomical use of the space provided, and that a suggestion of shelves (which she drew in) would help him to organise the complicated main area and door compartment areas. This paid off. On the four sets of shelves he has recalled an impressive number of items – not just butter, but low fat butter, fish fingers, corn flakes, cheese, orange juse [sic], milk, plain water, hot dogs and many more items besides. Throughout this drawing period his teacher prodded him on to better things: 'I'm sure that you can think of more things to put in your fridge than that!' With each new prod, new items appeared. As he progressed towards the inner doors, and seeing the greetings cards which had been made as part of another project on display, he asked if he could make his book have a birthday theme; hence the caption 'Happy Birthday to Alun on your spercle Day', in well drawn letter-forms; and 'Open to your surprise' on the inner door, leading to a pictorial birthday cake surprise in the inner space.

'The witch and the jewels' (23 × 17) by Alison (8)

In this project with eight-year-olds, the teacher brought in *bric a brac* from home and arranged it in the classroom, roughly four items to the group tables. To create an atmosphere, cotton scarves and remnants of material were placed as both surface for, and backdrop to, them. This arrangement formed a still-life group for the pupils to draw.

How the project was organised

Process

The pupils made their own books by following the instructions of the teacher:

Demonstration procedure

① *Hold the piece of paper in the landscape position.*

② *Now fold it in half, horizontally.*

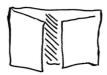

③ *Now fold left and right sides to the centre.*

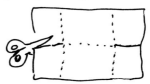

④ *Open the whole sheet and cut through the middle, but ONLY on the outside panels.*

⑤ *Fold on the horizontal again.*

⑥ *And fold the outer pages to the centre as shown.*

Cover and page design sequence

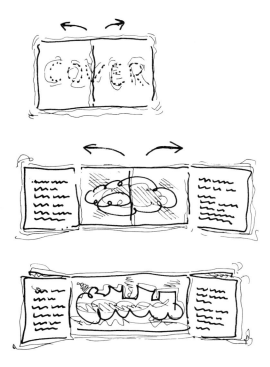

Part 1 – When opened to the first page, the extreme left and right flaps were reserved for 'story' and left blank. The two central pages were designated as the illustration area, and by supporting the book on a small board (of the clipboard variety), and holding it at an angle between the knee and the edge of the table, the pupils drew whatever composition was in their view. The divided centre to the page provided a design challenge because one has to either avoid 'crossing the gap' when drawing the objects, or place them in such a way that the edge doesn't disrupt the rhythmical action

of drawing. Alison avoided the problem by dividing the composition into two halves.

Stimulating the narrative

As the artwork neared completion, the teacher isolated periods of time to improvise stories linking the objects together; thus the illustrations provided a structure from which a narrative was envisioned. The planning and drafting of the narrative was made on A6 size copier paper so pupils could conceive the narrative in the same size as the book form. After editing each other's work the final version was copied in ink. Alison's story fitted neatly into two halves of the A6 outer folds, so she decorated the lower portions with other objects in the still-life group.

Part 2 – By opening up the inner two pages another set of panels become available for processing. At this stage (about two weeks later) each table group moved on one table to a new still-life arrangement of objects and continued the previous method when arriving at a completed page. There is no open edge to the centre of this book section, which accounts for the freer composition in Alison's central illustration. We can also see that her drawing skills have developed through the project. As can be seen by reading her narrative, she has succintly and imaginatively interwoven the Russian toy, the teapot and the plant.

So many themes, so many variations!

It is tempting to go on showing variations of books with moveable interiors made by children, and the

ideas they trigger in terms of written and visual content. Once the inside of books have their umbilical cord (that has bound them into the form for two thousand years) cut, a new era is thrust into view. That era is so young that we hardly know how to handle it yet!

Perhaps it is worth asking here how 'married' these paper forms are to their graphic contents. Couldn't any theme, in any subject, or area of interest be integrated into any book form? To some extent this is true, but some book forms, like the 'house and garden' books, seem to have an organic affinity with their theme. But there is another, less easily explained situation which arises when a new book form seems to be asking to be used. And that 'presence' never ceases to amaze me for, somehow, books and the ideas which are realised through them, seem to come together – meeting each other somewhere inside the imagination, and knowing that they are meant for each other. Perhaps books are made in heaven!

When eleven-year-old Péter finished the 3D buildings which illustrated his story, he thought for a while and then started to make sketches for a similar book, but this time on the theme of his hobby – aeroplanes. His teacher said, 'I don't think he needs any help from me now'.

There is something about being a book artist which makes one almost fanatical about inventing new books. It is partly caused by the paper bug, because once bitten, you are never the same again, but it is also the intuitive desire to invent something new, and then to be changed by what has been made. The American book artist, Hedi Kyle, belongs very much to this category, for she breathes air into the book anatomy in the work she produces. Referring to her experiments she says:

'Extreme angles, cut-out areas, shaped panels, and images broken by folds interacted with light and shadow. These contrasts heightened the effect and illusion of a stage setting or an architectural site. Pop-ups and panoramas based on Victorian models captured my imagination, but above all I was fascinated by the Oriental sensibility to transform paper into magical objects.' (1991)

There is something of this 'Oriental sensibility' in these book forms and something, too, of modern sculpture. The work of Barbara Hepworth comes immediately to mind. The 'holes' in her sculptures are of course not holes at all but sculpture which has air as its form. The bird in the eye travels through those negative shapes as they intertwine with the stone or polished bronze and a dance for two electrifies the space which holds them. If you make a slot in a piece of paper and weave another piece of paper through it – like the books which follow – there is a kind of Hepworthian spatial dynamic at work for one form is travelling *through* another. The possibilities in terms of paper sculpture and architecture are enormous. Here, only one aspect of the genre is discussed.

Slot book 1

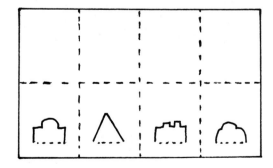

① *Crease landscape to eight rectangles and open. Cut shapes to bottom panels and crease at base.*

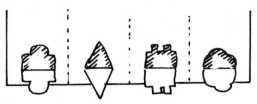

② *Drop top panels behind bottom ones. Hinge open forms and draw through base line.*

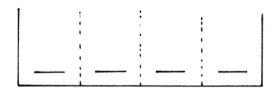

③ *Lift up engineered panels and cut lines on bottom sheets.*

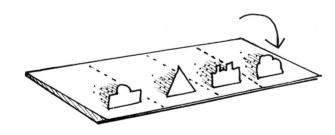

④ *Lay sheet down as diagram 1. Drop top panels over forms and lift them through slots.*

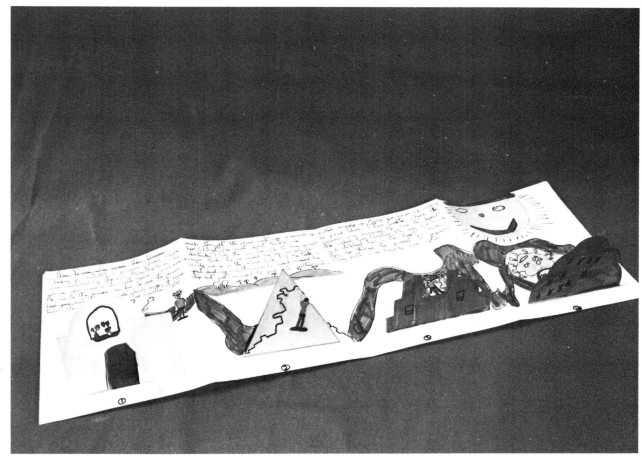

'The prince who saved the princess' (16 × 23) by Vicky (11)

This book exemplifies the first of the 'slot' books. It is viewed from the front and from above, with the 3D forms in the foreground, the artwork environment in the middle ground, and the text at the top of the page.

How the project was organised

The teacher planned the project for a third of the class (the other two groups were working on the completion of another book project). She cut the engineered forms and corresponding slots, (ensuring variety of design using the 'multiple cutting technique' (see page 114)) to cut down time.

Process

1 The group carefully slotted through the forms on their individual books. The style of presentation was introduced and discussed.
2 Horizontal lines, 1 cm apart, were drawn down each panel to a third of the length of the page. In this way the pupils could visualize, approximately, how many words could be accommodated in each section.
3 A brainstorming session followed, aimed at (*a*) providing images suggested by the forms, and (*b*) developing plot structures which could link them together in telling a story.
4 There was now a choice of starting points. Pupils could either (*a*) tell the story through artwork in the 3D form and environment, or (*b*) draft the narrative and, after editing, write it into the book.

Like most children, Vicky chose to draw the artwork first because the pull-through form was such an unusual and stimulating experience. Her plot, the archetypal prince-rescues-princess-after-overcoming-obstacles one, is told through a continuously winding path, in much the same way as many illuminated medieval manuscripts convey a narrative.

In Slot book 2 the 3D forms are moved from the foreground to the background of the page. This changes the whole design concept which is taken even further in Slot book 3.

Slot book 2

Design forms in top half of bottom panels. Follow previous instructions.

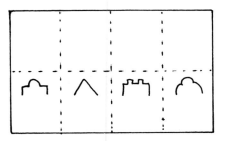

Slot book 3

The diagram shows that the engineered forms can be placed in almost any position and drawn through slots. Follow same basic instructions as before.

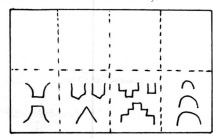

See **Terry's Journey** by Steven in the colour section on page 103.

Steven's book is an example of the genre taken to the next stage of development. Here the whole book is conceived as a horizontal 3D environment. Indeed, only the capacity to fold down into a concertina distinguishes it from a table-top sculpture. Of course, forms cut on three sides and hinged on the fourth are a very simple way of making a 3D form, but the problem with it is that a hole is then created by the negative space of the engineered form. The advantage of this technique is that the weaving process leaves the page arena untouched (apart from the slot), thereby enhancing the 3D design and leaving the flat artwork area uninterrupted.

Planning the project

The strategy for this task followed on developmentally from the previous one. Having decided on the narrative structure of the story, Steven sketched out the architectural features he wanted engineered. This is not as difficult as might be supposed because, as the diagram shows, they are drawn onto the panels as in a conventional picture. These forms can be placed anywhere, and indeed at any angle, because what is possible on the 2D area of the page can be realised in the 3D space above it.

Engineering task

There are no hard and fast rules one can make about children engineering paper with a craft knife, and I have more to say about this later in the book. In a model curriculum the development of these technological skills would be given far greater attention. Pupils can achieve quite astonishing skills of paper engineering with practice, for it is little different to learning to hold a pen and make it draw shapes on paper. Just as one learns to vary the pressure on a nib or pencil to strengthen or weaken a line, so one learns comparable skills with a craft cutter. One soon learns what pressure is required to cut cleanly through paper of different weights and qualities. Steven's engineering was partly done by the teacher, and partly by himself. If the whole process had been done by him, with several trials and many errors, it would have probably taken too long, and his enthusiasm for the project might well have been dampened. The same goes for the mathematical laying out of lines for writing on and margins. This is part of the development of ruler-using measuring skills, but it can also become a laborious chore if insisted on in every book-producing enterprise.

A subsequent task to the cutting one, is marking where the slots should be placed, cutting them, and then the dexterous task of feeding the engineered form through the slot into the area in which it is to be raised to a 3D position. Of course, the more complex, and the greater number of forms there are, the harder this is; but skills have a habit of developing simultaneously, so the more complex the design of forms, the more likely it is that the pupil will have the matching capacity to realise them technologically or, have the potential to do so. This applies to the teacher too: the more one uses a craft knife, the faster and more accurately one cuts. As a general principal, think of all these technological skills as being gradually acquired over years. It is neither necessary nor desirable that every skill should be addressed at once: indeed, such a policy could result in both teacher and pupil losing interest in producing a book.

Artwork

All the artwork (including the 3D forms) was done on the surface area. I asked Steven if the 3D forms got in the way of the pen and crayon work on the flat environmental surface. He said, 'No, it's quite easy because you can move the standing up pieces forward or backwards depending where on the page you are drawing'. I asked him what he liked about this kind of book and he said, 'I like the way that when you first open the book all the standing up shapes are lying down. Then, as you follow the path along you raise them to help tell the story until at the end all the shapes are standing up'.

Writing

Steven's story – again an archetypal one about a boy who goes in search of gold – has a complex plot. 'When I started to write, all kinds of new ideas came to me which I added on to the ones I had already thought about when I was working on the drawing.' The drafted plot was written onto separate pieces of paper and these, with an additional sheet to complete the story, were glued on to the reverse side of the book.

Slot book 4

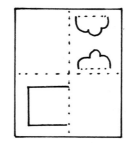

① *Crease vertically and horizontally on portrait. Engineer forms in top right panel and door in bottom left.*

② *Fold bottom pages under top ones. Lift forms and cut through horizontal hinge space on panel beneath.*

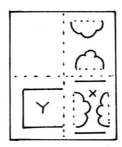

③ *Open sheet and cut forms 'X'.*

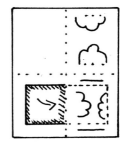

④ *Fold panel 'Y' under facing page.*

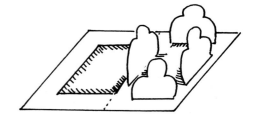

⑤ *Drop top panels behind bottom ones. Engineer forms through slots and raise forms 'X'.*

'Bogus' (16 × 23) by Peter (11)

This final example shows another variation of the genre. This was a collaborative teacher and pupil engineered effort. Shapes, at any angle, can be engineered through the slots, creating a total theatre of forms in the round. Peter's work – more in the form of a greetings card than a book – shows how the four panels of A3 size paper combine to make a sophisticated design. By engineering the inside left panel under the right side of the fold, and engineering the 3D forms from it up through the slots above it, one avoids the negative 'holes' which would otherwise appear on the back cover.

Esprit de corps

When I present children's self-made books at conferences and courses I am often asked if they have been made entirely by the authors concerned. Often, particularly with simpler forms, the paper technology has been the sole effort of the pupil, but with more involved forms the teacher has invariably had a hand – sometimes a big hand – in the construction process.

I am very much in tune with the notion of the teacher or parent creating alongside the child. The teacher who writes or draws out of his/her own personal need will feel affinity with children doing the same thing, and teach the better for it. That is why I aim to stimulate the reader to become a book artist first, and teacher of book art second.

To fall in love with the magic of paper is the first step to being a successful teacher of the book genre. Only then can one feel at ease with it and open the gateway into new forms of

communication for those who come into contact with us.

Purists will object to the teacher cutting and folding the book forms that children then process. But if doing this elevates the beholder to higher levels of cognition it must be for the best. In time, with love and patience, these sophisticated manipulative skills may well be mastered, the pupil becoming an accomplished communicator who, in turn, enables others to do the same.

A question often put to me is: How can a teacher spend so much time on the sometimes complex folding and cutting process with one individual, with thirty other children demanding attention? It is only rarely that I make a complex book form with individuals who are unable to construct most of it themselves. In those projects where one table is engaged on an activity which must be closely supervised, the rest of the class is involved on more conventional tasks, for example drafting the text or preparing the illustrations. Using pupils with basic technology skills to show others what to do is another invaluable teacher time-saving technique. One other way is to run a weekly lunch-time Book Art Club for those dedicated to it and so provide yourself with a team of assistants!

Finally, to illustrate the versatility of the 'cut and slot' style, two project books constructed in exactly the same way, yet containing two very different pieces of information are shown. The book forms themselves were given, ready engineered, to the authors (both seasoned book artists), although they had to weave the flaps through the slots.

Six-page slot book

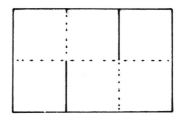

① *Crease landscape into six equal parts (almost squares) and cut as shown.*

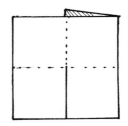

② *Fold right panel behind central panel.*

③ *Fold left panel in front of central panel.*

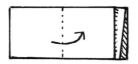   

④ *Turn book to landscape and fold inwards.*   *Plan.*

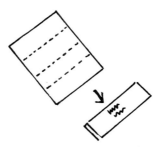

⑤ *Completed book.*

Page design

Draw in the engineering required on pages 2,3,4,7 and back cover.

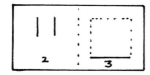

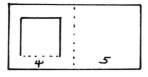

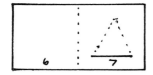

A letter/map/document is slotted through the cover. The book title is designed on the folded-down sheet and seen in the slotted area on the cover.

Open up book to flat sheet and engineer cuts. The door on page 4 slots through the slot on page 3, so these need to be lined up. The same applies to the back cover triangle and the slot on page 7.

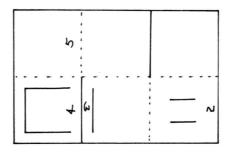

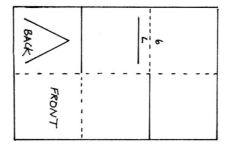

① *Document bearing title, shown slotted through the cover.*

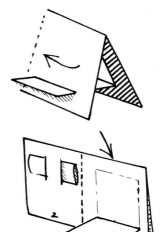

② *and* ③ *Square panel slotted through page 3.*

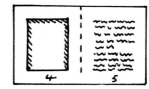

④ *Window mount created on page 4.*

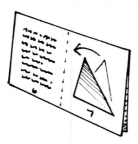

⑤ *Triangle slotted through page 7.*

⑥ *Back page window mounted area.*

Taking the book apart
To divide the book into two halves so that two pupils can work on it simultaneously cut 'X' (see below). This provides the following:

① *Pages 3,4,5,6.*
② *Front cover, pages 2,7 and back cover.*
   Glue strip to 'X' to return book to one section again.

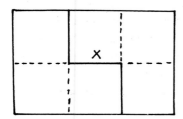

*See **The Hidden Treasure** by Sarah in the colour section on page 103.*

It would be unrealistic to expect a teacher to make thirty books this complex. It is a book style I reserve for those pupils who need a special challenge, like Sarah, who would regress if given the lesser challenge of a more standard book form.

How the project was organised

The stimulus of the map has appeared under a number of headings here and in this book it is the key pin around which the story revolves. The title is placed on the reverse of the map, and so by sliding it through tramlines on the title page, it provides the title of the book. The other 'slot' forms are used as 'before and after' devices rather than as 3D designs, hence on page 3 the flap is lifted to reveal something beneath it. However, the engineered form creates an attractive mounted area on the next page. This feature is repeated in the triangular forms on pages 7 and 8. This pattern of slotted-through pages is sandwiched by 'untreated' pages 5 and 6, so the whole book is an assemblage of treated and untreated pages, which the mind and imagination work on to make into a book.

Sarah's structure
Sarah works best when working on her own and usually has an outline plan for a new book almost from the moment of first turning its pages. Her technique is unconventional; instead of drafting each page systematically, she writes in undrafted

sentences (and sometimes just isolated words or phrases), entries scattered about the book. I have learnt not to interfere with this process, for a successful book has always emerged using this technique. It seems to be like sensing where isolated jig-saw puzzle pieces go on the board and then filling in around them until the picture is complete. This direct *in situ* approach does have its weaknesses; grammar, spelling and syntax often fall short of the narrative substance. But I instinctively feel that, for the moment at least, while this creative energy flows it would be counterproductive to 'improve' the mechanics of her writing in the process of authorship itself. Corrections can be done later just as I will check this page of text on the computer spelling check at the proof reading stage. It is much easier to correct spelling mistakes than to 'correct' uncreative writing. There is, alas, no known cure for unimaginative writing! There will be other ways, in other situations for concentrating on her secretarial skills, but I am adamant that this private space of her book is not the place for it just now.

Story outline
Finko contemplates sailing. He decides to have a go and, packing his 155 suitcases, sets sail. The ship sinks and he is shipwrecked, but is washed ashore on a desert island. He finds a shack on the island. The outside of the flap shows the exterior, and by lifting it the interior is revealed. In the mounted illustration on page 4 a periscope is drawn, seen by Finko as he looks out to sea. He then encounters pirates, but a knight in armour riding on a tortoise comes on the scene and rescues

him. Finko thinks he has found treasure but it turns out to be a theme park (this is illustrated by the interior of the triangular form on page 7). The story finishes with a firework display and the word 'congratulations' lighting up the sky. The back page synopsis (in the triangular-shaped mount) reads 'Finko is stuck on a desert island. Will he find the treasure? Or get drowned by the pirates? To find out read on!'

The map shows the main locations of the story. A key at the bottom of the page explains the meaning of these symbols.

Wonder homes!
This book is constructed in precisely the same way as the previous one, except that it has been taken to pieces so that two pupils can work on it simultaneously.

Theme
The book takes a satirical look at the brochures of the housing market. Various brochures for new homes were examined, and their contents discussed with the group involved in this project, so that the techniques of selling a house, and all the attractive offers made to the would-be purchasers, would be fully understood. Each page has a specific objective, described by a worksheet given to the co-authors, specifying the copy and artwork definition for each page:

See 'Wonder Homes' by Sarah R and Jung-Yul in the colour section on page 103.

Worksheet layout

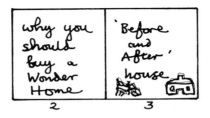

Jung-Yul's pull-out 'competition' is like Sarah's map in *The Hidden Treasure*. In it, the recipient discovers that he/she has won, amongst other things, five crocodiles, and the full *Encyclopaedia Britannica*! On pages 2 to 6 Sarah describes, with a confident design awareness, the advantages of buying a Wonder Home. The carefully drawn interior on page 4 is captioned 'This is what you get if you buy one of our houses!' But by the 'Special Features' on page 6 the cosiness of page 4 has turned to humour, for example, 'The house also comes complete with a huge hole in the roof'. Jung-Yul completes the brochure with pages 7 and the back cover. The 'guarantee' lifts to reveal an advertisement, and the framed area on the back page is reserved for the application form.

By this stage in this book, the reader should be able to break down into parts the communication and interactive skills which this project has developed. The three areas of text, visual material and the interrelationship of the two, invite analysis. To give just two examples, on the cover Jung-Yul uses the technique of diagonally presented words to 'hold' the reader (as discussed in Chapter 2). Later Sarah combines a graphic illustration showing the hole in the roof of the house with a reinforcing, yet minimal caption. Both of these techniques can be found in *The Jolly Postman*, *Marie Claire* and several million other sources of communication! They are as much part of our day-to-day 'language' as the basic, descriptive sentence, and are probably used far more often in the communications world.

Ecological books

'What kind of book is like a rain forest?'

Sarah

This chapter breaks with the pattern set by the rest of this book by starting, not with the architectural or anatomical aspects of books, but with the nature of their thematic content.

Most of us feel a helplessness when we watch nightly on television the destruction of yet another wilderness or hear the news that a particular bird or insect has just become extinct. I assume that I am not alone when I rage inside that such things can happen and that the cause of so much of it is poverty and the greed of unscrupulous profiteers, as well as the fact that the will of the West to prevent or change either seems so half-hearted.

Of course, ecological issues have a marked influence on many area of the curriculum, and rightly so, but some would see this as potentially counter-productive, as children are in danger of becoming so saturated with it all that they no longer really respond to it positively. Whatever the pros and cons of children engaged in environmental issues, the books which comprise this section have all grown out of a genuine concern for our world.

The above question, put to me by Sarah, set me searching through my repertoire of over a hundred book forms. Many of them could be *made* into tree

shapes, but I wanted a book which *was* a rainforest, if such a thing were possible. We (myself and a group of children) took some sheets of junk mail one lunchtime and began shaping this way and that. To make a form which crosses over itself, a profusion of shapes just like the rainforest, we soon discovered that a tripartite series of folds was needed . . .

Interlocking pages

'Trees' (10 × 17) by Sarah M (8)

This engineering technique immediately makes the form more interesting than a simple gate-fold form. Sarah has decided to draw the tree on the un-engineered side. Later, in more advanced form, artwork was placed on the other, engineered side. Although this is only an eight-word caption, Sarah spent nearly half an hour redrafting these words until she was satisfied. The first draft was 'If you like trees you will want to look after them won't you and not chop them down'. The reductionist process of caption drafting is evident in the copy she finally used – 'Please don't chop down trees. We need them'.

By folding down the outer folds into triangles and 'internalising' them one could not only double the number of interlocking pages but represent, to some extent at least, the conical structure of the tree . . .

Interlocking page book

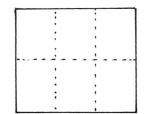

① *Crease landscape into six equal panels.*

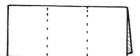

② *Fold on horizontal.*

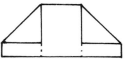

③ *Fold top corners to centre.*

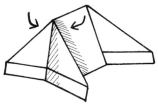

④ *Internalise side panels.*

The side-fold panels comprise four in number on each side. They can be arranged in a number of patterns, depending on what kind of information is to be communicated. In the most rhythmical sequence they are arranged as follows:

Page sequence

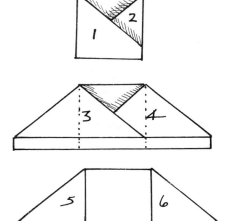

As a three-dimensional standing form the book can be presented in several ways:

Three 3D displays

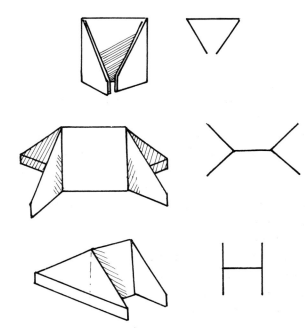

See **The Rainforest** *by Maeve in the colour section on page 104.*

The designing process

First of all, the book had to be visualised. Maeve made a mock-up of the book on junk mail, and then repeated the process more carefully, this time on lightweight cartridge paper. This was to be her draft book, the aim being to let the book form 'tell her what to put in it.' But when she started to draft her narrative she found the diminishing triangular space a distraction from the flow of ideas she was having. Instead, she drafted her plot in her drafting book.

Next Maeve decided on the arrangement of text and illustration and cut a template out of thin card with scissors to mark the inside border of all the triangular pages. This was planned out in the lightweight paper book, and then began the task of transcribing her story to the prearranged pages, using a pencil so that changes could be made easily.

She soon found that more skill is required in writing in a triangular form than in a rectangular one. The shape demands that you keep to its form; consequently some words just didn't fit. 'At the top of each page you only have a very small space -- just enough to write one short word, so I had to change some of the words to make them fit.' In fact, reading through her final book one can see just how clever she has been in arranging the text in the space, and one can only guess at the amount of rethinking that went into that refining task. Of course a computer can help with this, but how much more rewarding it is if your 'intelligent eye' can do it by itself.

The beginning of Maeve's story went like this:

'John stepped off the plane. He didn't like what he was doing at all. But he had to. Out came the cutting machines. Now all he had to do was cut down some trees. That wasn't bad was it? . . .'

Alex's book combines the engineered central panel of the basic gate-fold with folding and engineering of one of the side panels.

'Plant trees in the city' (10 × 18) by Alex (8)

Side-folded book

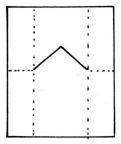

① *On portrait, crease left and right edges to centre. Crease horizontally on outside panels. Cut rising form in centre of top panel from half-way point.*

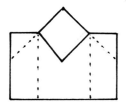

② *Drop top half over bottom half and crease corners on diagonal.*

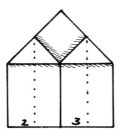

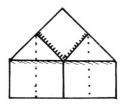

③ *Fold side panels to centre and internalise top corners.*

Middle section showing side panels open

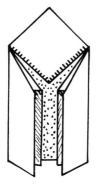

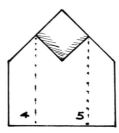

④ *Completed book.*

Inner section

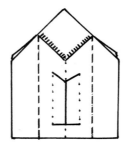

Adding extra pages to inner section

Page sequence

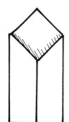

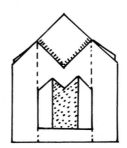

Cover

This book form is similar to Maeve's except that the pages do not interlock. Instead the process of internalising the side-folds on the triangle surprisingly creates two new pages. Thus a hinge effect is made down the centre of these pages which is a challenge to the designer. However, here it is not fitting words into a shape, but designing them to cross the hinge aesthetically, which represents the challenge. In Ruth's book, which follows, some lines of writing achieve this more successfully than others.

See **The Dying of the Rainforest** by Ruth in the colour section on page 104.

Ruth was given the ready-made book and she journeyed through it several times, opening up the pages as she did so, for she seemed as curious about its anatomy as she was about what could be placed inside it.

A time for immersion into a new experience is essential for the creative process to bear fruit. Like entering a new house for the first time, one needs a period of 'becoming acquainted' with all that is new before one can begin to 'make it one's own'.

Rainforest themes had been discussed with the class so Ruth already had a plot outline. I suggested that she leave the front two panels for the cover until the end of the project and plan out a sequence of ideas to match the inside of the two outer panels and the large, panoramic central spread. It was interesting to note from her draft that the first page of text was too long. The final sentence read 'The sun enjoyed shining and sometimes glistening drops of water fell from the

sky on to the trees below.' The redrafted version omitted the final five words without any loss of meaning. The right-side fold is a subtle blend of refined words and an image of a rainbow. 'Once in a while there would be a wonderful rainbow of glistening colours.' But her *tour de force* is the way she designed the text to continue to the unadorned back page for the sombre dying of the rainforest. 'The sun no longer wanted to shine and the rainbow disappeared. Everything was dead. The rainforest had died.'
This sensitivity to the meaning of emptiness on the page is a symbolic gesture we shall find elsewhere in these examples of children's expression.

Mariana's book combines most of the features already described. All three panels have been engineered creating, in this case, artwork illustrations to the four inner panels made on the two outside sections. The author-illustrator has gone to considerable lengths in celebrating the sheer richness of life found in a tree by her exuberant artwork researched from wildlife books. She concludes with a timely warning, 'Birds and animals that live in trees are dying every moment. Think about it!'.

Pop-up tree book
A book could be produced showing fifty different ways of using pop-up engineering to make a tree. This is just one of them.

The concertina folding of the foliage creates a spring reaction when the page is opened. All artwork should be done in the flat, then engineered, then finally glued into place.

Pop-up tree

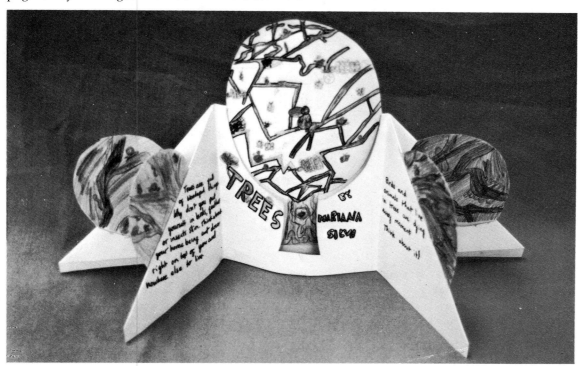

'Trees' (16 × 24) by Mariana (8/9)

① *Fold A3 landscape in half on vertical as pop-up base.*

② *Fold another A3 landscape on vertical and cut in half. This will become the pop-ups.*

③ *Take piece 'A', fold in half vertically, and cut away wedge shape (through both pieces).*

④ *This forms the tree branches.*

(5) *Fold up both sheets from the bottom at approximately 30 degree angle.*

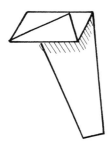

(6) *Fold at same angle and distance as before, but under.*

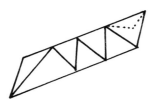

(7) *Continue this over/under pattern of folding until the strip is completed.*

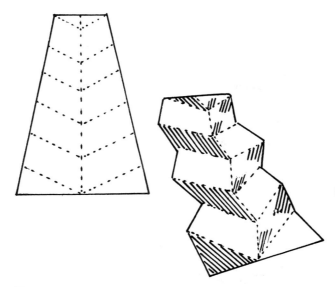

(8) *Open out the folds and the sheet should look like Diagram 8 (above left).*

(9) *Fold forms in a zig-zag pattern.*

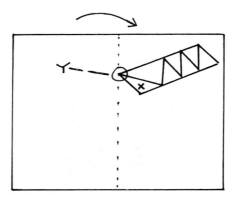

(10) *Fold the strip down flat and glue underneath panel 'X' to base. Point 'Y' should touch central fold. Glue top panel 'X', drop the left page of the base down over it.*

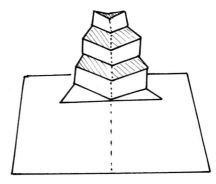

(11) *Wait until glue dries then open page to raise pop-up.*

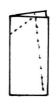 

(12) *Cut sheet 'B' in half on horizontal. On one piece, fold vertically on portrait and trim away two wedge shapes.*

(13) *The resulting form will become the tree trunk.*

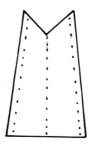

(14) *Open form and crease 1 cm left and right on side edges.*

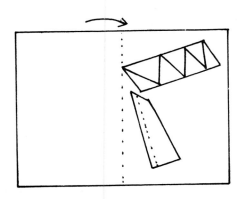

(15) *Fold on centre and lay in position just below form 'A'. Glue underside 1 cm margin to base. Glue top side margin and drop left page over it. Leave to dry.*

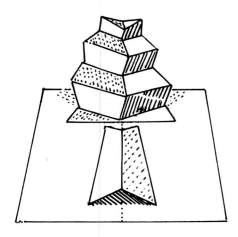

(16) *Open page to raise finished pop-up.*

'Save the trees' (16 × 23) by Emma and Tracy (8)

This pop-up book is part of a series of projects designed for classes of children aged from six upwards, in Manchester schools. The eventual aim is to make a pop-up ecology book made entirely by children.

How the project was organised

Making the flat pop-up forms is relatively easy. Templates were provided and then pupils drew around them and cut out the shapes. To introduce the theme I used David Pelham's wonderful pop-up book *A is for Animals* (1991) to stimulate the class. Although his book doesn't use the technique described here, it is full of creatures (including tree creatures) in their natural habitat. We listed how many creatures could be found in one tree, and came up with a long list of birds, rodents and insects. Then we discussed tree types and consulted a large chart showing their shapes and leaf forms.

Process

1 Working in pairs, one pupil used pencil crayons to draw the top, leafy part of the tree, while the other worked on the tree trunk form.
2 Paper for the base of the pop-up was distributed. Pupils drew around the raised trunk form and bottom part of the foliage form on this base.
3 Pupil 'A' drafted the copy for the left side of the base; pupil 'B' for the right side. A ten-minute brainstorming session came up with one-liners. Many were too long and were brought down word by word; others weren't interesting enough and needed 'energising'. The two in the illustrated example were typical of what was produced – 'Save trees. They shelter you when it's sunny.' and 'Save the trees. They give you oxygen.'
4 The final stage was the folding and gluing down one, by far the trickiest part of the process. The folding down of the leaf section was beyond all pupils but the gluing technique of both forms was understood by about a quarter of the class who helped the others, although finding exactly the right joining position proved tricky. (This stage was completed over several days of odd free moments and at lunch-times.)

The BUT book

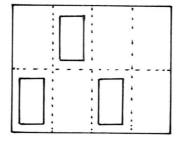

① *Crease landscape to eight rectangles. Cut window mounts.*

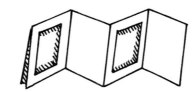

② *Fold on horizontal and concertina.*

The book can be processed on the landscape (table top) or portrait (hanging) position.

There is nothing innovatory in the technological form of this book. It is in fact the most basic book form of all – the concertina – enriched with window mounts to the illustration pages. The page sequence provides three 'double spread' pages, page 6 being the odd one out. This is put to good use here; in fact, the book concept pivots on this factor.

Hypothetical structure

1 Pupils select a word like 'but', 'because', 'suddenly', and design the word into page 6 of a ready-folded book. The word selected may well be conditioned by whether the book is in the landscape or portrait position, for some words will fit the orientation better than others.
2 The drafted text is then planned through two 'spreads' *before* the chosen word and one 'spread' *after* it. The challenge here is to plan a plot through two pages (each page has a matching illustration) to reach 'but' (or any other word), and to complete the plot after it.

There are some who would see this technique as gimmicky, but I think they are wrong. Try putting a plot together yourself this way and see just how much creative thought is required, especially within the prescribed refinements of a book like this.

See '*The Tree Queen*' by Anna in the colour section on page 104.

If a test of excellence is consistency of style, then Anna's book is a model of excellence. Every image on every page whether plot, handwriting, arrangement of words and paragraph structure, or artwork, border decorations and lettering, has a wonderfully harmonious continuity. The eye is conveyed effortlessly from form to form with the clarity of a successful communicator in the book arts. The basic plot is that the Queen of the trees is confronted by two men carrying wood saws. They plan to chop her down. BUT the Queen calls out in tree language for all the trees to move. The sudden movement of all the trees frightens the men away and they never return.

Tunnel book 1

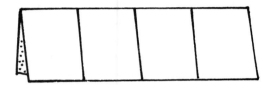

① *Crease landscape to eight rectangles. Fold on horizontal.*

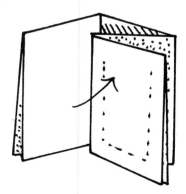

② *Fold panels as shown. Cut a door through the six right-sided pages.*

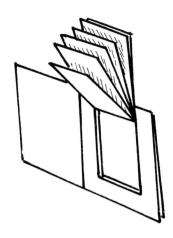

③ *Raise pages.*

This class of book comes in many forms and in two different styles, but here it is represented at its most basic. In its first style it is rather like a notepad in which the pages are lifted and folded over the top. An A2 sheet of paper is folded down to the A5 size. The cover is opened, and then the centre of all the right side pages are cut through on three sides so that they all lift upwards. (A sharp craft knife is recommended!)

*See '**What became of the rainforest**' by Ben in the colour section on page 104.*

As part of a whole term project on the eco system, Ben's brief was to design an environment awareness book. The book comprised six pages designed to be lifted upwards. He had already

written about the rainforests, but this part of the project was more to do with communicating the seriousness of the situation simply and briefly. The classroom was full of warnings from organisations like the World Wide Fund for Nature and Friends of the Earth, and the class was becoming aware of how important statements can be most effectively expressed in just a few words and a photograph or line drawing. So Ben set about making a crucial statement simply and to the point. 'I kept lifting the pages and trying to think what could go there,' he said.

He looked at a text book about the layers of undergrowth in the rainforests and how each species plays a crucial role in the survival of the 'community of plants' as a whole, and how many life-saving medicines are made from them. 'At first I thought I would use the layers of pages to be like the layers of plants in the rainforest and to have a different plant on each page.' But there was one problem with this idea. The last page opens out to nothing. How could that be incorporated into his ideas for the book? 'I kept thinking about it and then the idea came to me of using that last empty page – the *nothing* I mean – as meaning that something wasn't there any more.'

So Ben's ideas began to crystallise and before long he had composed a series of episodes in words and images which corresponded to the destruction of the forest. The artwork took up the whole of each page, with the captions written on the reverse of the page above it.

On the inside cover, Ben wrote 'The greatness of the towering trees that overwhelm the rainforest

are threatened. Look through this book and you will see the progress of the rainforest today . . .'
The rest of the pages went as follows:

1 'First the chain saws came in and cut down the trees . . .'
2 'Then the wood is exported to Japan . . .'
3 'Then the rest of the wood is burnt . . .'
4 'Then houses are made of the wood . . .'
5 'Now they have the house but what is left of the rainforest . . .'
6 Nothing (blank page).

The final act of lifting the last page to the empty nothingness beyond is one of those moments which induces an awe-inspiring silence whenever I present this book to an audience. Ben has hit on a great truth of communication with his book, and it is this:

> What moves most,
> and has the greatest impact,
> is what is stated in the middle of
> silence.

Tunnel book 2

In this second kind of tunnel book the pages open in the more conventional right to left direction. This differs from the previous book as follows: the book has 7 pages; the 'tunnelling' starts from the top page; the last page has not been cut; and the pages are hinged on the left side.

See **'My Cosy House'** by David in the colour section on page 105.

The project which stimulated this book was a

Tunnel book 2

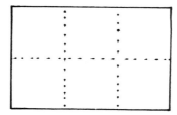

① *Crease landscape into six equal panels.*

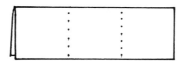

② *Fold on horizontal.*

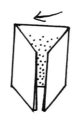

③ *and* ④ *Tuck right edge into left edge fold.*

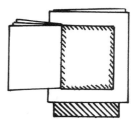

⑤ *Lay strip of card above the bottom sheet and cut a door through the other five remaining pages. The book is now complete.*

celebration of the good fortune it is to have a comfortable home. Comparisons were made with the poor living conditions of most people in the developing world, and the project focused on our responsibility towards them. So although this was not an environmental project as such, the underlying ethos was a very similar one.

Project organisation

The teacher made one book for each pupil. To underline our comparative affluence, the pages of each book made a tour of the pupils' homes. This was done by using a visualising technique. The first few minutes of each weekly 'book art' session were spent, eyes closed, as the class were taken on a journey into one particular part of their home by the teacher.

During the first week, the outside of the front of the house was the subject. The class were asked to 'see' the placing of windows and doors on the wall: Did the front door have a glass panel on it? Is there a door knocker or electric press button? A door knob, handle, yale lock? What colour is the door? Where is the house number? This line of questioning continued to include the downstairs window and what could be seen through it: the garden, or pavement, and pavement surface. In all, this must have taken about ten minutes.

Without any discussion, so that the images would still be sharp in their minds, the pupils could either draft a written description of the house front, or make a drawing of it. The drawing could be done directly on to the second, right side page of their books in light pencil, or on a piece of paper the same size as the page. More detailed pencil crayon work completed the task. The aim was that by the end of the morning session, both the left side text, and most of the right side artwork, would be completed. Book artists are expected to work hard!

This process was repeated weekly until rooms like the lounge, kitchen, bathroom and the pupil's own bedroom completed the book.

Between each session pupils were asked to take their book home, so that they could compare the visualisation with actual reality. This was most illuminating. In some cases whole walls of pictures and furniture had not been recorded; even things like their own highly decorated bedcover had been overlooked. Paradoxically, other parts of the house, like the toothbrush on the shelf above the bathroom sink, had been accurately defined.

Looking beyond ourselves

The class were asked what they thought would surprise, say, an African child visiting their homes. The response was:

Carpets on the floor.
Curtains at the windows.
Lots of things to pick up and look at like ornaments.
TV set and video recorder.
Books and magazines.
A fridge full of food.

If this project had done nothing else, it showed pupils how significant a home, and a comfortable home at that, is to personal happiness. The book recorded that recognition and also, that our domestic environments reflect us as people and our aspirations. The page of the book dedicated to the pupil's own bedroom was very relevant, as here was the space which most reflected his/her own sense of self, both positively – a money box for Ethiopia – and negatively, in owning things which were unnecessary.

The above paragraph might be termed the 'inner' meaning of the book, for whatever a book is about, and whatever techniques have been used to communicate meaning, one 'looks through the images to the reality beneath', for there lies the real truth of the matter. One could say that in the intellectual maturity to write and draw with fluency and conviction as demonstrated by these examples of the book art concept, our children radiate their good fortune. Taken a stage further it could be said that anyone – child or adult – who fails to do this is letting Western privilege down.

Analysing the cognitive processes

A great deal could be written in attempting to break down into examinable units what skills have been acquired by this project. By visually scanning reproduced pages from the 'Home Book Project' it must be clear to the questioning eye of the beholder that the detailed drawings of each room reveal a sophisticated handling of symbolic concepts. The text and visual imagery complement each other; the visualisation technique has opened a door to the memory resulting in a flow of written descriptions, and this in turn demands an enlarged box of literacy tools. There is a growing confidence with using perspective which, consequently, opens up the 'picture plain' to an expanded conceptual field of definition. Colour is used with increasing symbolic meaning, to show the differences between pattern, texture and shape. One could go on breaking down the classifications in, and achievements of, communication skills in this way. But it is the book form – a complete, pulsating organism – that enables so many skills to be processed with such interrelated directness.

Display books

The final book in this section, like so many discussed here, lies somewhere between what is a book and what is a paper environment. As will have been observed, I am intrigued by the techniques used by organisations such as banks, insurance companies and building societies, to advertise their services. I like to study their windows in my local high street and make sketches of what new folded paper construction is on view. The following is an interpretation of one such marketing object which I have adapted to classroom use.

Display book

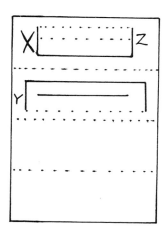

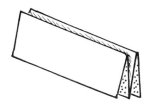

③ *Complete folded-away book.*

The visual effect of this 'presentation' is not unlike that of the cinema, with a strong, panoramic image as a 'stage', and a large foreground 'auditorium' suitable for a slogan.

Chris was given the ready-constructed form along with the challenge of making a warning about deforestation. It is possibly the most visual of all the projects shown in this book and

① *On stout paper (or thin card) crease four equal strips on the portrait horizontal. Cut panels as shown and crease dotted lines. Section 'X' should be smaller than 'Y'. The slot on 'Y' should be wide enough for 'X' to slot through.*

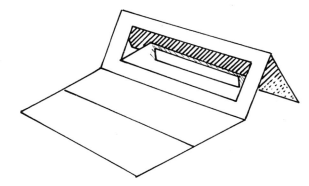

② *Fold first two panels into a triangular shape. Drop 'Y' forward and slot 'X' through it, folding the first crease 'Z' upwards.*

'The rainforest' (30 × 11) by Chris (11)

highlights the communicative powers of visual forms over words, which can often be inept. Chris, like his older brother Nick, whose work has been featured in one of my previous books, communicates visually with ease. In my experience, every classroom has a Chris – a pupil who is venerated by the rest as being 'good at art' – and so often we, as teachers, fail to embrace what they have to share with their peers.

I have always been uncomfortable with the idea of the teacher as the 'master' and the child as the 'apprentice', because it is simply a falsehood. If only our teachers *could* draw half as well as many a pupil, or string words together as imaginatively as children so often do. In the classroom situation we are all in the creative melting-pot together.

If you have pupils who have above-average skills in drawing, ask them to help you teach the others. I always do. What better technique in developing communication, confidence and inter-personal skills can there be than this?

Withdrawing from drawing
A teacher colleague who works with six-year-olds noted that some children in her class will draw in other pupils' books either by request – 'Will you draw a dog for me?' or as an uninvited gesture – 'Let me draw a dog for you.' She was concerned that this would lead to (*a*) a stereotypical way of drawing spreading around the class, and (*b*) some pupils withdrawing from drawing altogether, preferring to use the services of the 'artist in residence'. She eventually overcame this situation by using a visualisation technique in which the children drew familiar objects as she described them. She would ask: 'What does a dog's face look like?' and then from brainstormed 'drooping jaws' and 'floppy ears' build up a picture in the mind which was then transferred to paper in simple drawing stages. Although after these games some children continued to have some of their drawings done for them, there was a marked improvement in 'the sanctity of authorship', as the teacher described it.

'I've lost my . . .'
Three million schoolchildren every day of the year

The only advantage of working in an exercise book is that things don't drop out of it. The book art enthusiast – the person who sees that the book concept opens doors into the imagination held firmly shut by most other means of writing – has to enter the rich and wonderful world of the designer. That means that ideas will often find their way into the world through drawings, diagrams, rough notes on any piece of scrap paper lying around and photographs cut out of magazines or junk mail. Storing is essential.

Here is a folder designed with a number of pockets, made from a single sheet of paper. If each pocket is given a designation and labelled – for example, rough draft, cover designs, illustrations – the owner will know exactly where to find that which is required at any stage in the book assembly process.

Book art folder

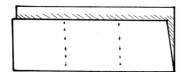

① *Crease landscape A2 vertically into three. Fold horizontally so that the back sheet is wider than the front one.*

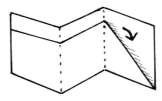

② *Tuck right front panel inwards on diagonal.*

③ *Turn to other side. Fold left panel to centre. Tuck right panel inside diagonal.*

④ *Completed folder.*
The fourth compartment is open at the bottom. Either glue base of opening, or avoid using it. There are still four other sealed compartments!

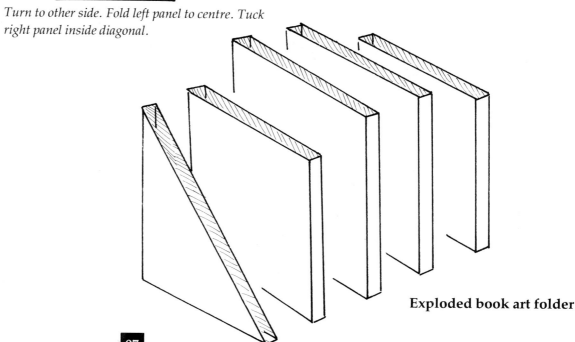

Exploded book art folder

'Rosie's Special Surprise Birthday' (10 × 15)
by Tara (5) (See page 24)

'The Birthday Party'
(30 × 22)
by Natalie (6)
(See page 24)

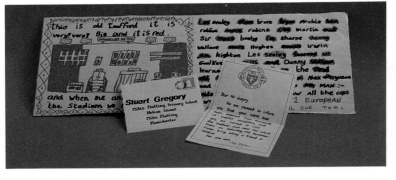

'The Letter' (21 × 15)
by Stuart (8)
(See page 26)

'The Mystery Wallet' (11 × 15)
by Amanda (9) (See pages 30 and 42)

'The Hidden Treasure
Hotel' (26 × 19)
by Rebecca (8/9)
(See pages 31–2)

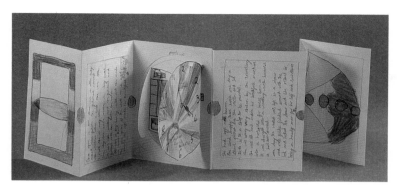

'Wristwatch' (16 × 11) by Rosie (8/9) (See page 44)

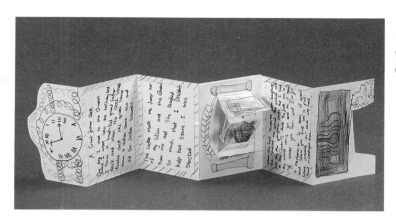

'A Grandfather Clock'
(12 × 8) by Sarah Jane (8/9)
(See page 43)

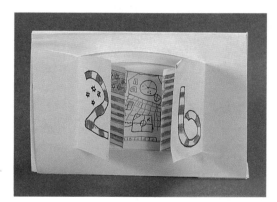

'26' (12 × 8) by Lawrence (8/9) (See page 44)

'The Lost Wallet' (16 × 11)
group work (10) (See page 46)

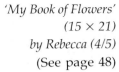

Cover

Back cover

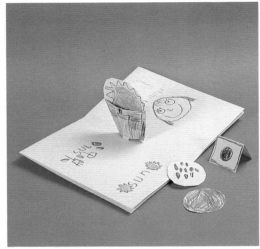

'My Book of Flowers'
(15 × 21)
by Rebecca (4/5)
(See page 48)

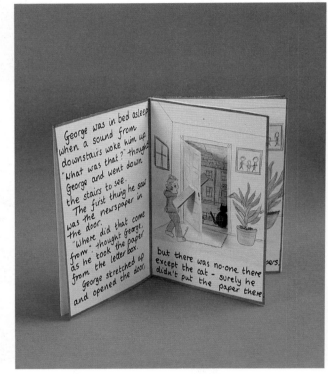

Page from 'George and the Letterbox' (11 × 16)
by Sally Kemp (See page 53)

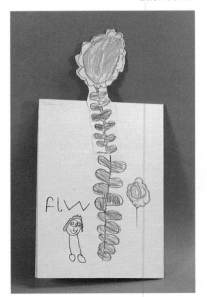

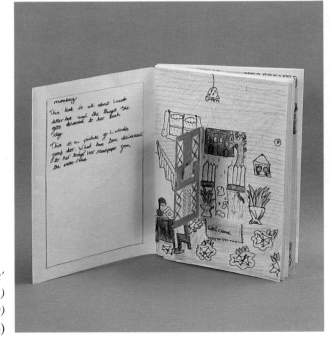

'Lucinda Letterbox'
(16 × 23)
group work (8/9)
(See page 54)

'Lucinda Letterbox' displayed

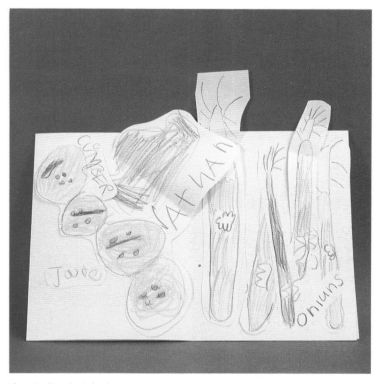

'Sam's Sandwich' (16 × 23) group work (4/5) (See page 56)

Covers of both books

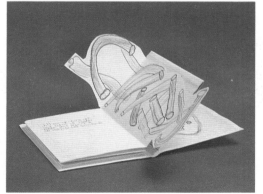

'Jill's Sandwich' (13 × 18)
by Rebecca (7/8)
(See page 57)

'Clean Your Teeth' (15 × 45) by William (7/8) (See page 60)

'Priscilla at the Dentist' (11 × 45) by Meinou (10/11) (See page 60)

'Silly People in Silly House' (14 × 17) by Shelly (10) (See page 70)

House exterior

House interior

'Mystery House' (23 × 19) by Patrick (6) (See page 71)

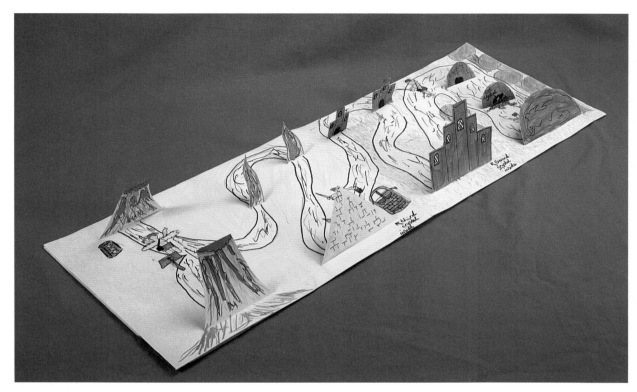

'Terry's Journey' (16 × 23) by Steven (11) (See page 78)

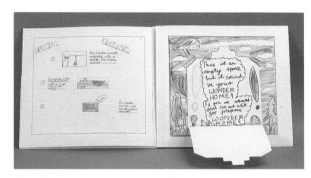

Selected pages from 'Wonder Homes'

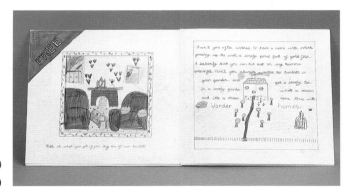

'Wonder Homes' (23 × 22)
by Sarah R and Jung-Yul (9) (See page 83)

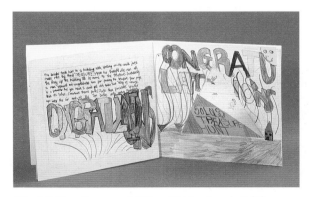

'The Hidden Treasure' (23 × 22) by Sarah F (9)
(See page 82)

'The Rainforest' (14 × 15) by Maeve (10) (See page 85)

'The Dying of the Rainforest' (11 × 19) by Ruth (10)
(See page 87)

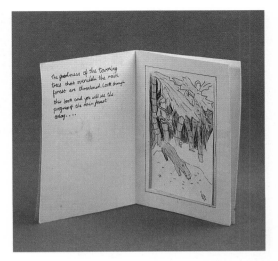

'What Became of the Rainforest' (15 × 21)
by Ben (11) (See page 92)

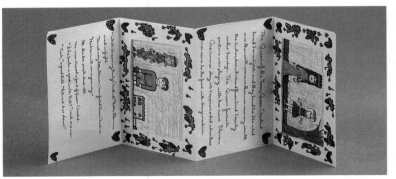

'The Tree Queen' (15 × 10)
by Anna (10)
Front (See page 91)

Back (See page 91)

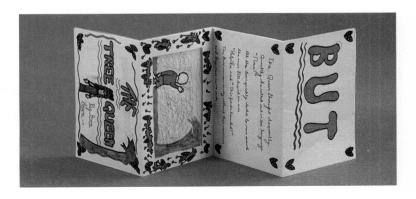

'My Cosy House' (23 × 22) by David (11)
Cover (See page 93)

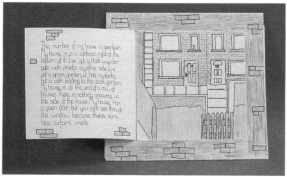

Front of house

'Mary Goes on Holiday'
(10 × 12) by Sarah (7)
A concertina book, with
accompanying paper
cut-out objects, housed
in a 'suitcase' box.

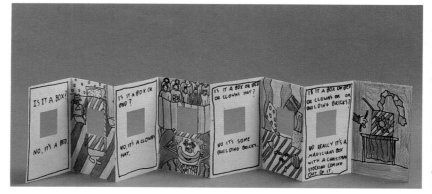

'Is It a Box?' (7 × 11) by
Alex (10)
A concertina book with
open square areas in the
centre of each page.
The task was for Alex to
make a 'Is it a . . .?' book,
linking illustration and
captions to a guessing
game strategy, with the
answer revealed on the
final page.

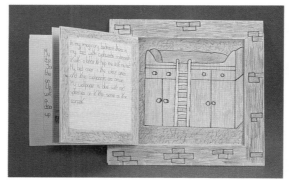

Bedroom

④ Book art – organisation and evaluation

'Man is at his best when he listens
to the voice inside him.'
(Old Japanese saying)

At the beginning of this book I implied that I hoped that the children's work 'contained within' would evidence that a new kind of linguistic and visual literacy can be realised through the book arts, and that although other seminal systems exist – the computer being one – nothing processes it better. Largely through anecdotal evidence (the reporting of how teaching friends and I have organised book projects), outline sketches have suggested how one might approach organisational strategies. A number of different approaches have been suggested from independent to collaborative work patterns; whole-class teaching to small group activities; projects designed for an afternoon's duration, or a programme extending over several weeks.

By focusing attention on the book as architecture, some things, regrettably, have been omitted. For example, I have said little about the curriculum context of this work; where and how it relates to other concepts of language teaching (reading, gender, sexism, racism, special needs, media studies) or the teaching of subject domains like history, geography or science. In time, no doubt, others will fill these gaps, as the book arts become more widely acceptable as a curriculum process

and specialists turn their attention towards them. Lack of space has also meant that continuity of learning through the book arts – how one book project leads to another developmentally – has only been implied in the text rather than given systematic attention.

Points about organisation and structure

The book form – technology

As a general principal, children need to have in front of them the complete, yet naked, book from the very beginning of a project. You have to know what a book is before you can 'write' one! So once the outline structure and reasons for making the book have been discussed, paper should be at the ready. Whether they make them unaided, aided by you, or you make them yourself, depends on what level they have reached on the technology skills ladder. If two or more pupils share a book producing project (like those on pages 30 and 90) the sharing of the folding, cutting, and refolding task can simplify the process. One technique I use with most classes I have worked with is to get every pupil simulating the book form they will be working in on A4 copier paper or even junk mail. Sometimes this is repeated before making the final form on, say, A4 cartridge paper.

Several of the book forms here, because of their complex 3D nature, will require substantial teacher input. But with regular practice, using a craft cutter skilfully is not that difficult, and many of these book forms would not be explored more than, say, once in a school year. Whether or not pupils use a craft cutter depends on their stage of development and the situation in which they are working. No hard and fast rules can be given for this, except to say that I try to introduce cutters to pupils at around ten years of age. Obviously, books which can be made entirely by using scissors (or with no cutting at all) cause fewer problems with pupil involvement, but craft knife cutting skills are an invaluable asset in technology work.

Conceiving, drafting and editing

After making the basic book form, a project can take several directions. The commonest is for pupils to plan the book's contents in relation to the technological framework in front of them. As can be observed from the children's work here, this usually involved alternating text and illustration. But as all these books are innovatory forms of graphic communication, each book really must be planned in its own unique way. One drafting technique I have used regularly over the years is for each table of, say, six children, to have a thin card template measuring one to two centimetres smaller than the page. They then draw around this in their drafting books for the draft, and later in their finished book for the final copy. This means that pupils draft in exactly the same space as the finished, margined page size.

So much has been written about the process of writing that it would be pointless to use valuable space discussing it here (see the book list on page 117). However, what most studies on the subject lack is attention given to the concept of writing *as design*. Studies in developing handwriting skills are becoming more popular (the pioneering work of Rosemary Sassoon is important here), but manuals on lettering and calligraphy tend to be decontextualised. Children preparing texts for presentation *is* part of their English education. I have made reference to this dimension of language frequently throughout this book, albeit briefly, but much more information needs to be made available to teachers in this area.

Art and design
To my knowledge, no one has ever written a book for teachers which examines in depth and breadth the interrelation of words and pictures in expressive learning. This is an appalling omission when so many books on teaching English and teaching art, published in the last twenty years, say much the same things!

The language of art in the classroom is well catered for in publishing and the books in the reading list should be consulted for information on approaches to drawing, colour work and experiencing materials. (Sadly, good writing on design education is not so plentiful.) What you

may well have to research yourself is where to use pictures, diagrams, maps and where to use story, written information, captions, or instructions. In the book arts we are all pioneers! I have found that children very often have an intuitive sense of what modality is best suited to a particular goal. Whether this is archetypal in a Jungian sense, or through the internalised experience of accumulated text book and mass media experience is open to debate. Strip-cartoon comics have done a great deal of unacknowledged teaching in showing pupils (mostly boys) how to explain often quite complicated events, situations and objects in basic words and images.

On a practical note, use soft pencils (2–5B) as they can easily be erased, as well as giving much more variety of texture to the marks made than harder pencils. Dry colour (pencil crayons, conte crayon) is more practical than paint for illustration work, particularly in a cramped classroom with thirty children. Pen and ink work is a compromise between the two and introduces children to one of the classical techniques of the genre. Fibre-tipped pens can be used expressively, but can also produce some of the most banal artwork ever created by children. Use cautiously.

Combining drawing, colourwork and writing in lettering and design is another book art area which needs a whole book dedicated to it. I have made references to it where appropriate. As with all aspects of book art, use the best of children's picture books to help you here. Discuss with children how the cover of a story book has been laid out into areas of title, author's name and artwork. They are by far your best guide.

Evaluation

No writer or artist would feel a sense of achievement if they failed to apply a rigorous self-evaluation to their work. This 'critical eye' is 'organic' – part of the creating process. Some makers may well feel the need to do this in a detached and systematic way, but most, I think, integrate criticism into the act of making. I know that as I was writing this book I was 'assessing' continuously what I was writing, but in an intuitive rather than self-conscious way. That visionary educator, Robin Tanner, summed it up well when he said that the arts involve us in choice, and that demands discrimination and, ultimately, rejection. In many of the accounts here of children at work in the book creating process, we have seen how, through the sensitivity and imagination of the teacher, children have been encouraged to redraft texts, restructure the design of pages, refine lettering, paper folding and illustration techniques. To borrow from the Christian Schiller quote at the beginning of this book, this learning is being absorbed, assimilated and digested, until it 'becomes' *part* of them. The more books children make, and the more they learn to select and reject within that process, the nearer they will get to making symbolic statements of a high order.

But how we as teachers learn to distinguish between what 'works' and what does not in the book arts is a life-long process. This book only scratches at the surface of what a book *can* be. We all need help in not only deciding whether or not children are developing skills, but how we assist the developing process. For this reason I am using the National Curriculum (UK) as the basis for assessing some of the basic skills associated with the book arts.

Book art can be divided into three main areas of the National Curriculum, namely English, technology and art, but as it is subject to review, it would be unwise of me to refer to it in detail. However, the underlying trends in education, as reflected by the National Curriculum documents, are as useful a starting point for evaluating pupil achievement as any other.

English

The book arts address all aspects of English from speaking and listening to developmental writing skills. Nearly all the book projects discussed here are 'performable'. The process of taking letters out of envelopes and reading them to an audience *is* a performance. (Much more could have been said about what happened to these books after completion, for its construction is only the first stage of what a book is for.) Whether 'performing' these 3D books to one's peers, to a younger audience, or even to oneself, one uses skills, including drama, in a most unique way. Of course, all the more fundamental exchanges of discussion, brainstorming, improvising stories and delegating tasks are integral to the book-making ethos.

Chronological and particularly non-chronological writing skills (both given attention in the National Curriculum) have been a focus of this book. Indeed it could be argued that the English attainment targets at key stages 1 and 2 are nowhere more 'deliverable' than through the book

arts in general. Assessing language skills in cross-curricular book art projects would therefore apply National Curriculum criteria in all its areas.

Technology

In essence, attention is given to pupils being able to conceive a design, organise and plan the making process, and evaluate the functional outcome. Technology and design in the book arts can be categorised under two main headings:

1 Constructing the book form (selecting the form, folding, cutting, assembling).
2 Designing the contents (laying out page grids, handwriting, lettering, illustration).

Both simultaneously stand apart and are interrelated. The book form is a model system of related parts which are combined for a purpose (all the books shown here communicate information to an audience).

Illustration enables pupils to explore and use a variety of materials. Assessing pupils' abilities then, centres on how well they can fold, cut, arrange and conceive the 3D form and the skills of page design in writing, lettering and illustration.

As with English, practical uses of the subject are underlined: a range of graphic techniques and processes should be experienced, like planning an advertising leaflet and understanding how advertising helps to promote and sell goods (plenty of examples are given in this book!). Evaluating and testing ideas, designs and artefacts should be a continual process at every stage of production (for example, asking your partner if he/she can tell what is going on in your illustration).

Pupils should learn to work in a team and to delegate responsibilities (for example, group book-creating projects).

The skills of making 3D models are given particular status. One might say, in all seriousness, that the book arts are a model of National Curriculum technology in action. When critics of technology, as it is implemented in many schools, describe it as the 'Mickey Mouse curriculum', they reveal that they certainly have not been to any of the schools represented in this book! It is common to think of paper as a trivial technology material and for 'real' crafts to be in metal, wood and plastics. Anyone who thinks that, should turn the pages of the new books on paper design work like Paul Jackson's *The Encyclopedia of Origami and Papercraft Techniques* (1991), to see what a fallacy that is. In fact, you can do more with paper than almost any other material, and as part of a 'whole class' programme of learning it is unsurpassed. If it is used trivially by some teachers, it is because they have not had the opportunity to experience its language fully.

Art

There is necessarily an abundance of cross-over between art and technology. It reflects the trend for pupils to see their own expressions in the light of the work of other artists, craftspersons and designers. Pupils learning to 'read' illustrations in their illustrated books, and the design of books in general address this effectively. Pupils making and investigating through drawing (observational and imaginary), mixing colour and exploring texture and pattern is well provided for in their own book-illustrating and cover design. In fact it is debatable if a better model could be found than illustration and 3D page design to enable children to 'explore, apply and experiment with ways of representing shape, form and space.'

'It is well to remember from time to time that nothing that is worth knowing can be taught'.
(Oscar Wilde)

Teachers live in an evaluation-saturated educational ambience. A lot of what is expected of teachers in this area is, I believe, counter-productive and unnecessarily time-consuming. Clearly we must know what a book is capable of becoming to make one, as well as understanding what skills children need in order to make one in all its parts, and how those skills are developed. The best evaluation system of all comes from intuition growing out of an immersion in the subject (the 3D book) and closely observing children at work. Consulting evaluation manuals serves at best to sharpen one's thinking, to ask questions about how you determine what needs to be changed and plan for the future. But if you 'listen' to the books your pupils make, they do tell you how the next one can be better. Moreover, I find that children themselves when asked something like 'What could you have done to make that illustration more interesting?' will say the same as your own thoughts about it. With wonderful books like *The Jolly Postman* and *Sam's Sandwich* around, children not only find inspiration, but a model form of communication against which to test the success of their own work.

Now assessing the strength of one's vision can be a technique in itself. In extreme cases we throw away everything we do in disgust at its failure, or we think what we have produced is beyond improvement. More often, we don't really know what a 'good' example of what we are making should look like, or even if we do, how to change what we have made to make it look 'good'. Copying others' work leaves no lasting sense of achievement. So what are we left with? Getting better at anything is a very slow and arduous task, as I have found to my cost. It takes time to be really fully aware of what it is you are trying to say and the techniques you use for saying it. Peeling away the lies we tell ourselves is part of the way forward. The rest is learning to look *through* one's writing, drawing, design work to what *could* be there, and that word *could* is the key word, because only a gradual growing knowledge of communication skills can fill that emptiness beyond your marks on the blank paper with ideas. The more I teach, the more I am sure that successful evaluation of pupils' achievements can only come from this gathering of, and sensitivity towards, the language of communication. One must be a maker before one can be an evaluator.

⑤ *Systems old and systems new*

A professional designer friend once said to me:

> 'A graphic designer is only as good as his design skills when his computer has broken down.'

'A spaceman came down to scare me' (18 × 15) by Sam (5)

a spsman cm dn to scr me.

Sam

Few books can be written about aspects of education today without reference to information technology. Yet I find to my surprise that it has not played a role of much importance in what has been explored in this book. This is primarily because the book as architecture induces the imagination to extend to the third dimension. In some sophisticated forms the computer is adept at simulating 3D environments, and is much used by architects and interior designers in this respect, but for most uses of the electronic image in our primary schools at least, its function is a two-dimensional one.

If you have worked alongside the diagrams in this book or, better still, have gone one stage further and invented your own book forms, you will have discovered that the art and act of folding paper creates a processing language of its own. By that I mean that the tactile shaping of paper suggests ways in which ideas and feelings can be expressed which are *hidden from view* in the flat form. Of course clay or fabric can be modelled into 3D forms relatively easily, but neither material has a history of writing attached to its surface. This is where the magic of paper lies, for its familiarity to us as a receiver of language means that it is natural to perceive it as a holder of surface images. Hence words and images are lifted into a 3D consciousness when a book – even a blank book – of the third dimension is made.

This book has been about what that phenomenon does for communication. Of course, computer-processed words and images can be used in a 3D book, but this book has been about the *transformative nature* of the third dimension on graphic coding systems.

There are two dynamic processing systems of our time. One is a very new system and still relatively expensive: the other has its roots in antiquity and is relatively inexpensive. One is universally lionised, the other as yet barely recognised. I am referring, of course, to the computer and the book. Even in processing the most basic of information the computer operator has to think in a new way. The multiplicity of choice of how one can prepare information on the screen has forced all of us, often unwillingly, into becoming designers. This has come as quite a shock to many who, believing that they are 'unartistic' now have no choice in the matter of designing a page. There is a myth – something of an escape clause – that the computer somehow does the design for you, but a glance at all those posters and notices in public buildings and private offices shows how mistaken that notion is. What the computer reveals more than any other communication system is how bad we all are at design. In the old days of the scrawled fibre-pen notice one could get away with appalling lettering and positioning of words, but the electronic eye shows up our visual insensitivity glaringly. Good design is in the mind, not the computer. At last, we are beginning to see that design is the means by which what is to be stated is done in the most visually appropriate way possible. The word 'visual' is the most painful concept for the curriculum to swallow, but the two great communication systems under discussion here are nothing if not visual.

Now the resourcefulness of the computer miracle is good news for education, always trying to force a quart into a pint cup, but there are some problems with it. One is, as medical research has shown, that extended exposure to a computer screen can be harmful. Also, there is evidence to show that concentration levels diminish after a relatively short period working at a computer screen. However, most teachers would see the biggest problem with the computer as an economical one. The financial hardship of our state primary schools suggests that it is unlikely that every child will have ample computer experience for some considerable time to come; indeed it may prove idealistic that such a notion were ever possible. If there is only one computer to each class, or less, progress in processing information and using it as a creative tool will be retarded.

So how do children process so much information using so many different techniques in the crammed curriculum? Thankfully, fate has provided schools with another dynamic processor of information – the book. It contrasts with the computer not only by being very old, but also by being, in its mechanical structure at least, very simple. If the computer is astonishing by virtue of its complexity, the book is equally astonishing because it is made solely of pieces of paper hinged together. On one level they have nothing in common, and yet on another level they complement each other wonderfully, for the elder statesman bestows his wisdom on the younger thinker of genius. New ways of thinking, as in so many walks of life, are fired by the classical forms of the past. In return, these great institutions (if they still remain), like the book, are energised by a new transforming power. There can be very few writers today who do not construct their texts and, where appropriate, graphics, on a computer, yet it is the book concept that is still the driving communicating force.

The journey the book has taken in two thousand years is one of the most enthralling stories of civilisation. But what is it that makes the book so new and able to stand alongside the computer in status terms? The answer in part lies with what has been the subject of this book – the innovative 'architectural' concepts of children's picture books. A book is no longer a passive experience but an active one in which the reader is a participant. Designers, writers and illustrators of children's books have broken free from classical structures to create new book forms of meaning. And yet it is one of the oldest book forms of all – the wonderful paper inventions from the East, the origami connection – that is at the centre of it all. Every child in every school in the world can have a dynamic Zen-inspired system in front of them in seconds. As we have seen, these archetypes are the source of a never-ending flow of new book forms and communication possibilities.

The advantages of the book form do not end there. Whereas children must wait their turn for the computer, there is no such delay in making and processing a book. Unlike the computer, the child is not only involved in constructing the book's contents, but in making the form of the process as well. Nothing is plugged in. A book can't break down. It never needs servicing and (provided it is cared for with love) never has to be replaced; indeed, in a deeply personal way it is irreplaceable. Apart from writer's cramp and wrist fatigue, caused by holding a pen, pencil or crayon too long, there are no stress-related symptoms associated with making books. The book doesn't make distracting buzzing sounds, neither does it need a special area to house it. However enlightening and time-saving computer graphics are they can never compete with the experience of dancing a soft pencil over a surface, or the

'Is it a box?' by Alex (10) being explored by a six-year-old reader

sense of the word. But to plan the cover of a book with drawing instruments on a sheet of paper is equally important. Professional designers can do both. The book and the computer are not in competition with each other but are partners, each showing another way of solving a problem; each compensating for the weakness of the other; each combining to illuminate communication.

Publishers are well aware of the psychology of the book; that we like the feel of paper in the hand; that the book is symbolically a mother form and that we cherish our books as if they were somehow part of us. Is it going too far to say that the book humanises the computer? Perhaps it is, but there is some truth in it. One may send a word-processed letter ending a relationship, but never one proposing the start of one. Advertisements promoting gold-nibbed fountains pens sell not so much the pen as the words of love such a sensual object will stimulate in the writer, and the effect it will have on the reader. Whether we are ready to accept it or not, such things lie at the heart of our personal happiness. Paper speaks with its own voice. Ignore it and there is a breakdown in our survival. There must be a balance between what we give to our society as work, and what we need to give to ourselves as emotional and spiritual sustenance. We hardly want our children to become the neurotic technocrats we can so easily become ourselves.

The sensual book of gracefully folded paper, of things you can take out and put in, of pop-ups and pull-outs, of paper book-sandwiches and book-toothbrushes can't provide this balancing trick unaided; but assisted, it is a great harmoniser not

sensuality of line that only a moist sable brush can give. Nothing on earth can replace the delight of feeling real ink flow from a beautifully crafted pen or the effect pastel gives on textured paper.

Yet the magic and mystery of computer graphics can stimulate children in unprecedented ways, and word processing can give children who 'hate writing' a new lease of life where writing with a pen has failed. As words appear on the screen they instantly have an air of authority, like words in a published book, and so the confidence to communicate is given a boost. As pupils learn to control the ways words can be arranged on the screen, so they become designers in a very real only of the curriculum, but in the life of anyone who cares to use it. A deputy head recently invited me into his secondary school to set in motion a cross-curricular book-creating project. He said that as his pupils developed into young adults their only concern was how to get good grades; what they learnt, or the joy which comes from 'making' something was irrelevant to them. He hoped that personal pleasure would be generated from making books, and that this in turn would result in a love of learning. William Morris referred to 'the beauty of life', a state of being in which every activity was marked by beauty through design in the very widest sense of the word. Parents and teachers know that when children make something themselves using good quality materials, it helps to develop good handwriting style, writing confidence and drawing and design skills, which in turn motivates them to want to learn more.

Providing the book form is taken seriously – for it is easy to treat it as a novelty – the impossible task of teaching so many subjects and communication skills to so many children may not be so impossible a task or so daunting a prospect.

'Will you please make me a book to work on at home'
(More children than I could ever remember)

Page from Beowulf (21 × 30) by Sian (11)
(The old and the new. Ancient-looking manuscript combining word processing on a computer with free-hand drawing.)

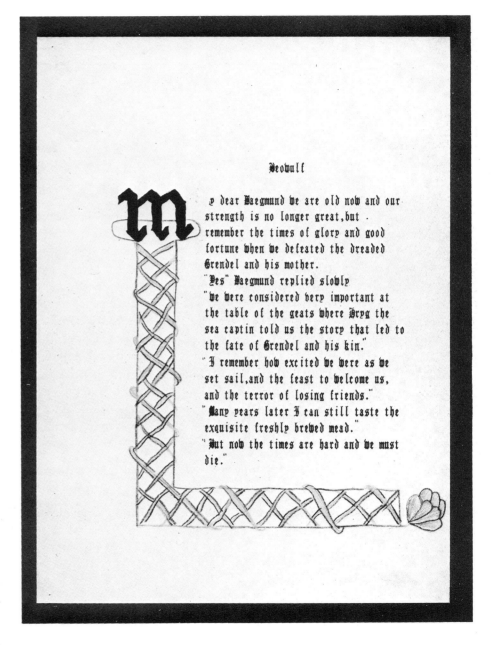

● *Appendix 1 – Constructions with paper*

Paper

The renaissance that paper has experienced in the last few years now means that books on working with paper are appearing daily. My notes about it here are brief, only addressing those aspects of the material and of shaping it which will be useful to the novice book artist. Cartridge-type paper comes in weights: 80–100 grams = lightweight; 120–200 grams = medium weight; and anything above 300 grams = heavyweight. I like to use lightweight paper (even newsprint) for experiments (the lightweight cartridge is then saved for recycling), but nothing less than 130 grams for the finished article. As you will see from the next section, good quality paper, especially bought in relatively large quantities, is not as expensive as is commonly imagined.

Paper sizes

This is stating the obvious, but the size of the sheet of paper used to make a book determines page dimensions when folded down. Clearly a book with eight pages will have smaller page sizes than a book with four pages. So it is essential to decide the size of paper before commencing a project. Always experiment on copier paper or junk mail and then decide from that the most appropriate paper size – A4–A1 (or the equivalent). (See Appendix 2 for notes on paper suppliers and commercial sizes.)

Folding and cutting

Accuracy in folding is essential for a well-made book. Aim for sharp fingernail creases. These will be easier to fold and also to see when you come to cutting them. Cutting a straight line with a pair of scissors is a technique worth practising (for both you and your pupils), and is part of book art knowledge. Another equally important skill is that of using a craft cutter. This essential piece of equipment will, with experience, make light work of 3D book making. Use a steel ruler to achieve a straight cut (an advantage that knives have over scissors) and hold the craft knife in an horizontal position (don't point the knife down and use the point).

Multiple cutting technique

This is a simple and time-saving way of cutting a design on several sheets of paper at once. Draw the pattern to be cut on a 'master' sheet. Use bulldog clips to attach this to three other sheets of the same size (the 'heavier' the paper, the fewer the sheets). Cut through all the sheets using the master as the guide.

Basic book forms

Basic origami book

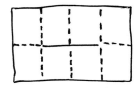

① *Crease to eight-page landscape. Cut through central panels with a craft knife. (Alternatively, fold on vertical and cut through middle panels with a pair of scissors.)*

② *Fold on landscape horizontal.*

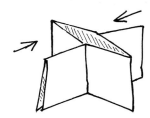

③ *Push book ends to centre, creating a star shape.*

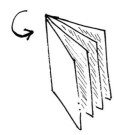

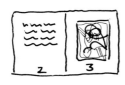 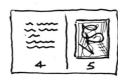 

④ *Wrap around pages to make a six-page book.*

Hidden staple book

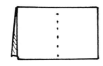

① *Fold three or more sheets of A4 on portrait horizontal and then crease on vertical.*

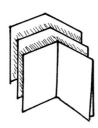

② *Superimpose them as folded pages.*

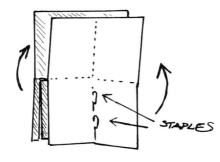

STAPLES

③ *Raise the outer sheet of the back folded page, and inner sheet of the inside folded page. Staple through the spine of the bottom sheets.*

④ *Drop down again the raised inner and outer pages.*

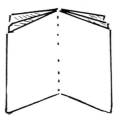

⑤ *The book is now joined together and the staples are hidden! (To make the cover stronger use a heavier grade of A4 paper.)*

Appendix 2 –
Paper, materials and equipment suppliers

Craft cutters

Available from most art suppliers and DIY shops. Cutters with retractable and replaceable blades are recommended.

Cutting mats

Expensive but virtually indestructible
small – CM30 (30 × 45cm)
medium – CM45 (45 × 60cm)
large – CM60 (60 × 90cm)
Recommended, large mat for staff use, medium for general or classroom use. Catalogue and price list available from:
Edding (UK) Ltd, Merlin Centre, Acrewood Way, St Albans, Herts, AL4 0JY (Tel: 0727 46688). Generous discounts to schools.

Steel rulers

30cm safety rulers for small work but 1m for cutting A1/A2 sizes of paper. Safety Rulers available from:
NES Arnold, Ludlow Hill Road, West Bridgford, Nottingham N62 6HD (Tel: 0602 452200).
1m rulers available from DIY shops.

Adhesives

Most PVA adhesives are suitable for basic books. Available from educational suppliers and DIY shops. Recommended: Marvin Medium from: Berol Ltd, Oldmedow Road, King's Lynn, Norfolk PE30 4JR (Tel: 0553 761221)

Recycled paper

Most schools find inexpensive recycled quality art papers difficult to come by. However at least one company will supply it providing it is purchased in minimum quantities of 5000 sheets. Forming a group of five schools in your area and each taking 1000 sheets is a practical way of economic bulk ordering. However, note that bulk orders can only be taken from one school, on one account and delivered in total to that address. Check that deliveries can be made in your area and confirm current prices. Some out-lying parts of the UK may necessitate special carriage arrangements.

Renew Matt white 135gms SRA2 (packaged in 500 sheet packs) contact:
Brands Papers, Park 17, Moss Lane, Whitefield, Manchester M25 6FJ (Tel: 061 766 1335)

Paper from natural sources

Send stamped addressed envelope for lists of Maureen Richardson's handmade plant papers and details of her paper making courses.
Maureen Richardson, Romilly, Brilley, Hay on Wye, Hereford HR3 6HE (Tel: 0497 3546)

Non-recycled paper

Cheapest source probably your LEA Supplies Department if there is one or NES Arnold (address above). Recommended: 115/135 gsm cartridge SRA1 (640 × 900mm) and SRA2 (450 × 640mm).

NB. These sizes are slightly larger than the A1 and A2 measurements but can be used proportionately in the same way, e.g. for A2 sizes read SRA2. Alternatively, paper can be cut down to A1, A2 sizes (A1 = 594 × 841mm, A2 = 420 × 594mm).

For wide range of papers including end of line bargains offers and discount to schools contact:
R.K. Burt and Co., 57 Union Street, London SE1 (Tel: 071 407 6474)
Falkner Fine Papers Ltd, 76 Southampton Row, London WC1B 4AR (Tel: 071 831 1151).
Wide range (including Japanese and marbled papers). Price lists and samples available.

● *Book list*

Children's Books

The following books have been selected because they illustrate aspects of the designs represented in this book, but have not been referred to in the text. They are not necessarily the 'best' of what is available, but a personal selection by the author.

Books with removable paper objects

Beastly Birthday Book   Babette Cole and Ron Van Der Meer, London, Heinemann 1990
This book includes removal aerosol ('Rhinoderent'), song book, pop-up treasure chest, underpants, and tinned fish (Loch Ness Salmon), all hilariously combined by the inimitable Babette Cole.

Griffin and Sabine   Nick Bantock, London, Macmillan, 1991
Like *The Jolly Postman*, this book has 'real' letters in envelopes, but the mood is surrealistic and more appropriate for adults than children. It looks forward to new ways of defining relationships between people in the genre of the visual novel.

The Fantastic Fairy Tale pop-up Book   Anon, London, Harper Collins, 1992
An impressive sequence of 180-degree pop-up forms with removable miniature books on each page.

Cops and Robbers   Janet and Allan Ahlberg, London, Heinemann, 1978 (Reprinted 1989)
This Ahlberg book includes a list, map and poster but in drawn form and provides an insight into the Ahlbergs' thinking, which led up to the movable objects within *The Jolly Postman* (1986)

Lift-the-flap books

There must now be several hundred books using the hinged door or lifted flap technique. The following have been selected:

Who's at the Door?   Jonathan Allen, London, Orchard Books, 1992
The story unfolds through dialogue in balloons which is told first on the left page, and then on the inside of the corresponding opening door progressively through the book.

Knock! Knock!   Colin and Jacqui Hawkins, London, Walker Books, 1990
A popular book with children, it is full of macabre doorways into dungeons, Egyptian tombs, coffins and ghost-filled wardrobes.

Books using various 3D, quasi 3D, or experimental visual devices

Ghost Train   Stephen Wyllie and Brian Lee, London, Orchard Books, 1992
An atmospheric book employing the use of holograms.

Bow, Wow, and You on the Farm   Lisa Marsoli and Stacie Strong, Swindon, Child's Play, 1992
By inserting two fingers into finger puppets engineered on the back cover, a child can project the characters forward through slots in the book's pages and so perform the story as a piece of theatre.

Hatch, Egg, HATCH!   Shen Roddie and Frances Cony, London, Orchard Books, 1991
This touch-and-feel action flap book uses real string to simulate spaghetti and pieces of fabric to tell the story of an egg which is reluctant to hatch.

The House   Monique Felix, New York, Stewart Tabori and Chang, 1991
A delightful wordless book in which a mouse converts the pages of the book into a paper house. The bare, greyboard cover has a mouse hole cut into it. If ever there was a book about the transformative nature of paper, this is it!

Books with irregularly shaped pages

Zebra Talk   Vanessa Vargo, Swindon, Child's Play, 1990
A simple yet powerful book expressing the plight of the zebra by representing its stripes in stark black and white cut pages on irregular dimensions and including bullet holes.

Foot Book   Angelique and Maria Kounis, London, Treasure Trove Publications, 1990
A family is described through their feet sizes represented as progressively growing feet. The book's spine represents a ruler measuring increasing feet lengths.

Other selected reading

Children's literacy and handwriting

The Art of Teaching Writing   Lucy Calkins,
Portsmouth, USA, Heinemann, 1986

Writing with Reason   (Ed.) Nigel Hall, London,
Hodder and Stoughton, 1989

On Being Literate   Margaret Meek, London, The
Bodley Head, 1991

Becoming a Writer   The National Writing Project,
Walton-on-Thames, Nelson, 1989

Handwriting   Rosemary Sassoon, Cheltenham,
Stanley Thornes, 1990

Working with paper

The Encyclopedia of Origami and Papercraft Techniques
Paul Jackson, London, Headline, 1991

The Art and Craft of Paper   F. Shannon, London,
Mitchell Beazley, 1987

Children's art and design

Art in the Primary School   John Lancaster,
London, Routledge, 1990

Starting Design and Communication   Brian Light,
London, Longmans, 1989

Art 4–11   (Ed.) Margaret Morgan, Oxford,
Blackwell, 1988

Drawing to Learn   Dawn and Fred Sedgwick,
London, Hodder and Stoughton, 1993

References

ADAMS, P. (1973) *There was an old lady who swallowed a fly.* London: Child's Play.

AHLBERG, J. and AHLBERG, A. (1986) *The Jolly Postman.* London: Heinemann.

AHLBERG, J. and AHLBERG, A. (1991) *The Jolly Christmas Postman.* London: Heinemann.

BAKER, J. (1987) *Where the Forest Meets the Sea.* London: Walker Books.

BANG, M. (1985) *The Paper Crane.* New York: Greenwillow Books.

BJORK, C. and ANDERSON, L. (1985) *Linnea,* Stockholm: R and S Books.

BRIGGS, R. (1982) *Fungus the Bogeyman.* London: Hamish Hamilton.

BUCHLER, P. (1986) *Books.* Cambridge: Kettle's Yard Gallery.

DEWAN, T. (1992) *Inside the Whale.* London: Dorling Kindersley.

DIMENSIONAL ILLUSTRATORS (1991) *3-Dimensional Illustration.* Rockport: Rockport Publishers.

GOODALL, J. (1975) *Creepy Castle.* London: Macmillan.

GOREY, E. (1982) *The Dwindling Party.* London: Heinemann.

HADE, D. (1991) 'Being Literate in a Literature-Based Classroom'. *Children's Literature in Education,* 22, 1.

HEDGECOE, J. and VAN DER MEER, R. (1985) *The Working Camera.* London: Angus and Robertson.

JACKSON, P. (1991) *The Encyclopedia of Origami and Papercraft Techniques.* London: Headline.

KAISER, B. and WELLS, M. (1986) *Noisy Norman.* London: Blackie.

KYLE, H. (1991) 'Conservator and Book Artist'. *New Bookbinder,* 11 (London).

MACAULAY, D. (1988) *The Way Things Work.* London: Dorling Kindersley.

MARIE CLAIRE magazine (July 1992). Published by European Magazines Ltd, London.

MASON, L. (1989). *A Book of Boxes.* London: Orchard Books.

MCKEOWN, F. (1991) *A Hundred Acres.* London: Medici Society in association with Channel 4 TV.

MEEK, M. (1988) *How Texts Teach What Readers Learn.* Stroud: The Thimble Press.

PELHAM, D. (1990) *Sam's Sandwich.* London: Jonathan Cape.

PELHAM, D. (1991) *A is for Animals.* London: Macmillan.

PELHAM, D. (1992) *Sam's Surprise.* London: Jonathan Cape.

PEVSNER, N. (1943) *An Outline of European Architecture.* Harmondsworth: Penguin.

RUTH-STEPHENS, R. and ENIK, T. (1988) *Alf Hides Out.* New York: Checkerboard Press.

SALAMAN, N. (1984) *Cleanaway!* London: Pan Books.

SMITH, D. (1984) *Great Buildings.* London: Purnell Books.

SMITH, P. (1982) *The Book: Art and Object.* Merstham: C.P. Smith. p.6.

WILKINS, F. (1982) *Books.* London: Batsford.

WYLLIE, S and PAUL, K. (1990) *Dinner with Fox.* London: Orchard Books.